D0214448

RACE IS ABOUT POLITICS

Race Is about Politics

LESSONS FROM HISTORY

Jean-Frédéric Schaub

Translated by Lara Vergnaud

PRINCETON UNIVERSITY PRESS

PRINCETON & OXFORD

Copyright © 2019 by Princeton University Press

© Editions du Seuil, 2015. Collection La Librairie du XXIe siècle, sous la direction de Maurice Olender. First published in French as *Pour une histoire politique de la race* by Jean-Frédéric Schaub

Requests for permission to reproduce material from this work should be sent to Permissions, Princeton University Press

Published by Princeton University Press,
41 William Street, Princeton, New Jersey 08540

In the United Kingdom: Princeton University Press,
6 Oxford Street, Woodstock, Oxfordshire OX20 1TR

press.princeton.edu

All Rights Reserved

LCCN 2018930582
ISBN 978-0-691-17161-6

British Library Cataloging-in-Publication Data is available

Editorial: Brigitta van Rheinberg and Amanda Peery
Production Editorial: Sara Lerner
Production: Jacqueline Poirier
Publicity: Jodi Price

This book has been composed in Miller

Printed on acid-free paper. ∞

Printed in the United States of America

10 9 8 7 6 5 4 3 2 1

To Rebecca, Martha, and Jean

Later I came to know this gentleman much better and more closely, and therefore I have involuntarily presented him now more knowingly than then, when he opened the door and came into the room. Though now, too, I would have difficulty saying anything exact or definite about him, because the main thing in these people is precisely their unfinishedness, scatteredness, and indefiniteness.[1]

—FYODOR DOSTOEVSKY, *THE ADOLESCENT*
(TRANS. RICHARD PEVEAR AND LARISSA VOLOKHONSKY)

Lepidus: What manner o' thing is your
  crocodile?
Anthony: It is shaped, sir, like itself, and it
  is as broad as it hath breadth. It is just
  so high as it is, and moves with its own
  organs. It lives by that which nourisheth
  it, and the elements once out of it,
  it transmigrates.
Lepidus: What colour is it of?
Anthony: Of its own colour too.[2]

—WILLIAM SHAKESPEARE, *ANTHONY*
  AND CLEOPATRA, ACT 2, SCENE 7

CONTENTS

[xi]

RACE IS ABOUT POLITICS

The Current Moment

THIS IS NOT a history book. Or rather, this book does not only provide a history of the formation of racial categories in Europe and its colonies. The reader holds between his or her hands a collection of proposals on the ways historical research can contribute to contemporary debates on the attribution of racial identity to individuals and populations. The racial question looms on a global scale.[1] On the one hand, Western countries, whether or not they led colonial empires in the nineteenth century, must now deal with manifestations of racism, be they instances of police brutality in the United States, torrents of racist speech in a Europe confronting a migrant crisis, or "chromatic" social hierarchies in Latin America. On the other hand, interethnic violence and social fragmentation into castes based on ideologies of purity and heredity appear to exist on every continent. Nonetheless, this book focuses solely on Western societies, in Europe and the Americas, in order to avoid premature conclusions or approximations about situations that can be observed in Asia and Africa and that call for studies of those places specifically.

This book was initially written for a French-speaking audience with the aim of illustrating to what extent the French case is singular compared to experiences in other countries and to theories developed within other academic traditions. I hope that the American edition of this work will play a similar role for the American case. In the following pages, Anglophone readers will discover an analysis drawn from a historian's perspective and should note that my academic background does not mirror the usual approach to these subjects in the United States, and even less so do my proposals.

The method proposed in this work consists of identifying a core, which is specifically racial, within the collection of prejudices, phobias, political programs, and norms that are qualified, somewhat vaguely, as racist. Because *Race Is about Politics: Lessons from History* is not a history of racial thought, but rather an invitation for open debate to all readers interested in this field of study, its three primary objectives reflect a programmatic dimension. These objectives are as follows:

1. To distinguish racial categories and processes of racialization within a much larger group of xenophobic attitudes and policies;

2. To propose a chronology of the formation of racial categories in the West that dates back to the Middle Ages and is therefore not limited to the nineteenth and twentieth centuries;

3. To prepare students, citizens, and scholars within the social and human sciences to confront any challenges that may be created by the unpredictable outcomes of research in the field of genetic biology. It is, of course, indispensable to continue to denounce the ideological agenda and racist policies espoused by sociobiology. However, we must acknowledge that as the human and social

sciences continue to develop their respective expertise, it is critical to monitor what genetic biology may contribute in the future to our understanding of the development of man within society.

A Situated Perspective

This book makes proposals, which I am offering from within a specific time and place. At the same time, these proposals are underpinned by a methodological rejection of relativism. On the critique of relativism, we can go quickly. Suffice it to borrow from the anthropologist Gérard Lenclud a logical argument against the idea that there are between human societies incommensurable realities that are therefore incommunicable. When a researcher says that a word, a ritual, a cultural expression, or a social institution is untranslatable into the language of his or her own society, we assume that he or she first has understood these objects in their own context. If we say that social realities are incommensurable, it is because we have been able to measure them.[2] Thus the attribution of untranslatability and immeasurability to any object is a logical contradiction. Nonetheless, as the author of this book I have to clarify what my own historical and social coordinates are. Born, raised, and trained in France, I am a French citizen of second generation by my father's side and third by my mother's side, both of them having come from Jewish families, one of which migrated to France from Poland, and the other from Germany, before World War II. There is, of course, a direct link between my interest in racial issues and the memory of the Holocaust that has been central in shaping my personality. Knowing this, I do not interpret the whole history of the West as a long-term preparation of the final disaster of the Third Reich. My approach to political processes of early modern and contemporary eras depends on my anchorage in the European experience, particularly in France. I admit, but only to a certain extent, the argument that only those who have experienced some type of phenomenon are able to transcribe it, but not that only a certain type of people is capable of understanding the transcript. My experience in France taught me that there was not necessarily a difference between a Jewish sensibility and a non-Jewish sensibility concerning the memory of the Holocaust.

A recent book has shown it was exaggerated or even false to claim that silence was imposed in France concerning the Holocaust just after World War II, before the historical research on the genocide of the Jews changed the intellectual landscape starting in the 1970s.[3] It is necessary, in fact, not to be deceived by the retrospective illusion that past experience is made of silences, occultations, and amnesia. For those who have being willing to read testimonies, books, and articles, neither the genocide of the Jews nor the extreme brutality of the colonial wars was unknown in the 1940s, 1950s, and 1960s. Some historians of the late twentieth century composed inventories of silences that never existed. Thus, the practice of slavery until its abolition by Victor Schoelcher in 1848, the brutality of colonization in Africa (denounced by Albert Londres, André Gide, Louis-Ferdinand Céline, Léopold Sedar-Senghor, Aimé Césaire, and Albert Memmi), the anti-Semitism of the Vichy regime, the practice of torture in Algeria, racist killings committed in metropolitan France during the three decades following the end of the War of Algeria: none of these historical realities was hidden by a State's censorship. Undoubtedly, restrictions have been imposed, particularly in school curricula and television broadcasting. The main reason some historians have fabricated the narrative of occultations is that they wanted a set of themes not taught at university and in high schools to be explained, as opposed to other phenomena that cause less tension.

For those who wished to accept it, it was possible to be exposed to the revelation of all that in the history of France related to racist practices. It is also true that, for those who did not want to hear about it, these realities could have emerged from the individual and collective consciousness. That is why, after I have placed myself for the readers within a time, a place, and a family heritage, I think the critical work that is at the heart of the humanities and social sciences on an essentially open field carries much more weight in the work that I lead than what comes to me from my personal existence. I assume that the antirelativist flavor of the above remarks may fall within the scope of a universalist paradigm, which some critics have identified as the mask of political domination. For now, suffice it to say that there is no correlation between the radicalism of claims for equal rights and adherence to a relativistic rhetoric. Frantz Fanon's universalistic perspective, as a thinker and as an activist, still remains an admirable demonstration of this.

As I write this in 2016, France suffers from a number of internal tensions. This historical situation encourages researchers in the humanities and social sciences, including historians, to think about the shaping of racial categories. An incident that occurred on television on September 26, 2015, during a popular talk show seems indicative of what is now at stake in France. A politician, Nadine Morano, former minister in Nicolas Sarkozy's government, explained three times that France was a "Judeo-Christian" country and a "white race" country. A member of the neo-Gaullist party, she sheltered behind the authority of General de Gaulle, presenting her definition of France as a "white race" country as a quote from de Gaulle. Obviously, this phrase immediately aroused great indignation even in her own party. The racist far-right leader Jean-Marie

Le Pen applauded these remarks. The expression "white race" belongs to the vocabulary of only small groups of racist activists, called today "Identitaires," but not the neo-Gaullist party nor the National Front itself. In reality, the reference to de Gaulle was not straightforward: the supposed quote was reported by an assistant of the general over thirty years after it was delivered to him during a private conversation. As the conversation was later described by de Gaulle's biographer, the French president would have defined France as a "white race" society shaped by a Christian tradition.[4] But in 1959, this idea specifically meant that a country like France could not offer citizenship and nationality to the Arab and Muslim masses of Algeria. Therefore, if de Gaulle expressed this sentiment, it was meant as a mental preparation for the inevitability of the independence of Algeria. For de Gaulle, in a typically Jeffersonian move, the independence of Algeria was better for France than was the integration of native Algerians into French citizenship. Therefore, de Gaulle was preparing public opinion for the idea that the independence of Algeria was inevitable, or rather desirable. Since then, for far-right activists, France was ultimately humiliated when, after recognizing the victory of Algerian nationalists in 1962, it didn't avoid the presence of millions of citizens and inhabitants coming from Muslim North Africa. If one can draw an analogy, this is similar to the permanence of African Americans on US soil after the abolition of chattel slavery in 1865. In the current context, Morano, then, has deliberately created an amalgam between the current response to jihadist terrorism, the Islamophobia that is itself closely linked to the detestation of Algerian immigrants since the French defeat in Algeria, and the anguish caused by the arrival of Syrian migrants in the summer of 2015. In the time since these lines were written for the French edition of the book, political developments in Poland, Great Britain, and the United States have brought xenophobic and racist opinions out of the margins, and politicians have legitimized them in elections, conducting openly xenophobic campaigns.

Historians do not direct their research on the racial question according to the latest news. However, regardless of their preferred period of study, historians cannot approach questions of race without considering the triad of Jim Crow laws, Nazism, and apartheid. All scholars who explore racism share these points of reference whether they are explicitly recognized or whether they remain implicit and sometimes even unconscious. This is why, when applying the best historical methods, these historical phenomena should not be considered as the inevitable outcome of a long history that scholars attempt to unravel by following the thread backward. We should, on the contrary, consider the Jim Crow–Nazism–apartheid triad as the point of departure for any critical approach to a historical legacy—in other words, the political and intellectual context—that has concerned scholars of the human and social sciences even before they began studying race and racism. When historians of any period compare their specific case with contemporary racism, in order to demonstrate how their respective case resembles it or, on the contrary, is distinct from it, it's better to possess an in-depth understanding of how contemporary racist policies were established and developed. Consequently, historians of questions of race must be specialists in their respective periods and, at the same time, be equipped with a consequential knowledge and understanding of Jim Crow laws, Nazism, and apartheid. That is not always the case.

Racism as Politics

Broadly speaking, racism is distinct from all other expressions of hostility toward others by the fact that it identifies people and groups by what they *are* and not by what they *do*. Pirates, heretics, rebels, and hereditary enemies are typically victims of segregation and persecution because of the way they act or because of what they have done. Yet the distinction between being and doing, once examined within the context of the humanities and social sciences, appears quite fragile. One wonders in the name of which analytical method it is possible to separate what people *do* from what they *are*, that is, as two distinct planes of human existence, if not precisely within a framework of racist thought. Nonetheless, it's worth contemplating what this use of the verb "to be" (what someone *is*) signifies. Here, it implies a collection of attributes as disparate as: phenotype or physical resemblance to one's forebears; gender; native language; sexual preference; place of birth or upbringing; socioeconomic milieu; and, a recent phenomenon in the history of human societies, allegiance to a nation. These attributes share two characteristics: First, almost all these features are inherited, which is to say they are the result of a more or less perfect process of reproduction from one generation to the next. Second, attributes thus received at birth are difficult to change, in the sense that people cannot easily reject them or be painlessly stripped of them.

In other words, judging people for what "they are" equates to defining them by that which appears to be, at first glance, scarcely modifiable, if modifiable at all. What's more, once you define what people "are" through a process of identification— understood here as an externally imposed action—you are solidifying the inalterable, unmoving nature of their traits. The persons who define others in this way often do so for their own political ends, because they are simultaneously molding a self-serving hierarchy of elements that the identity of the "other" must include: gender, genealogy, religion, language, sexual preference, phenotype, accent, and so on. Little wonder, then, that mechanisms that characterize human beings according to race, or if preferred, genealogy and appearance, are often compared to mechanisms used to assign identity according to gender, class, and sexual preference. All these attributes benefit (or suffer, depending on the perspective) from limited alterability.

However, the aim of this book is not to examine the historical evolution of definitions of being, that is, what people "are," even within a precisely situated social group, as that would entail engaging the entire spectrum of the humanities and social sciences and perhaps beyond. On the contrary, the current period can be characterized by the confrontation between defenders of the mutable character of individual attributes and those who maintain that some level of inalterability exists. This unique historical context necessitates a few preliminary remarks. The notion that some part of what individuals inherit at birth can remain fixed is now strongly disputed. Indeed, the constructivist approach to human existence, which has been included in humanities and social sciences curricula for over a century, seems to have finally gained favor in both the political and legal arenas. An individual's native attributes are no longer definitively assigned. Gender (and even sex), physiognomy, sexual preference, relation to the past, and native language are now considered to be malleable, or more precisely, unable to be stripped of their malleability. We can reasonably interpret this state of affairs as the culmination of a process of emancipation via individuation.

In European and American societies, those who qualify hypostasis and homosexuality as crimes, or who claim that interracial marriage is a blight on a family's or community's honor, are not operating from any sort of moral high ground. In reality, their indignation comes from seeing that the field of mutable attributes has grown to the detriment of the somewhat supernatural sphere of the immutable. "Liquid modernity," according to Zygmunt Bauman's expression, is made of un-binding and disaffiliation, on the one hand, but it does not necessarily abolish the possibility of racism, on the other hand. But this evolution cannot be considered solely as the end to a continuous line of progress, or, in other words, a fundamental good. The problem remains: for a society of individuals to function over time and allow people to project themselves into the future, it is necessary that rules and values be stabilized, be they actual laws, or beliefs of a metaphysical nature. In the same way, once a critical analysis begins to break down all forms of affiliation or belonging, it will perforce discover that individuals prefer to band together by affinity or obligation. This is because, in reality, social life only rarely resembles a fantasy in which subjects voluntarily adopt any number of attributes that suit them depending on circumstance and mood. One of the central themes within the humanities and social sciences, and perhaps beyond, is precisely the challenges to a subject's free will encountered in the social sphere. The contemporary humanities and social sciences have dispelled many illusions of the reputedly immutable character of the attributes that define individuals and groups. The fact that we consider it legitimate for everyone to define him- or herself at all times according to his or her conviction and his or her feelings of the moment does not mean that society functions only as the encounter of an infinity of free wills in constant mutation. In other words, even within the framework of an individualistic conception of society, structures and norms unfold at times and in rhythms that are not the immediate desire of each. Thus studying social and political relationships is about understanding how individuals and groups combine their individual and collective inheritances and aspirations with those of other communities in a relationship that is not free from the past and that cannot confuse the future with the expressions of desires and fantasies. Conflicts are the expression of the opposition between interests, identities, inheritances, and projects. It is within this very general framework that racial discrimination is mobilized as a tool of domination or as a weapon of defense against processes that seem to threaten the interests and identities of racists.

The triumph of the plasticity of belonging should have favored the extinction of racist thinking in contemporary societies—an expectation that is, to say the least, off the mark. That observation is unsurprising, even though, as shown in the following pages, we are often reluctant to admit that racial definitions of individuals and groups are meant to challenge their ability (or right) not to correspond to the stereotypes assigned them. When people conform to the conceptions others have of them, meaning they maintain the role to which they've been assigned, there's scant need for a racial theory to express hostility toward them. The victory of mutability lies in offering individuals the possibility to *not* correspond to the image of the group into which they have been placed. The stigmatization of African Americans reached its racist peak when they obtained citizenship; homosexuals in France, upon demanding the right to be integrated into the common family norm, recently became a target. As will be seen in the following chapters, the main paradox of racism is that the rejection of the other is a response to the anxiety caused by the gradual erasure of differences between the dominant population and minority groups.

Racism from the Humanities and Social Sciences

From the perspective of the humanities and social sciences, the current period can be characterized by a paradox. For the last sixty years or so, researchers in the humanities and social sciences have admitted, consensually, that race as a biological reality that determines the variety of humans has no relevance when analyzing human societies, either in relation to their internal cohesion or to define what distinguishes one from another. In other words, while on the one hand the question of race must occupy a very important place in the study of social and political relations, on the other hand most scholars reject the idea that humanity is divided into races whose members bear the characteristics attributed to each of these supposed races. This constructivist model views race as a social and cultural artifact, and not as an underlying physiological reality. This is the only model on which studies by historians, sociologists, anthropologists, political analysts, and philosophers are based.[5] These researchers' approach is reinforced by the fact that geneticists themselves reject the concept of race. Biologists in fact resist the use of the term "race" because of its vagueness. Indeed, the notion of race, a combination of physiological concepts and social characteristics, proves useless when describing relevant distinctions between human beings.[6] Nonetheless, the prevention of genetic diseases relies on the identification of at-risk populations, meaning it relies on the probability of the presence of certain genes within certain populations rather than in others. And common sense tells us, based on an image repeated a thousand times, and verified a thousand times, that children resemble their biological parents (and grandparents). Researchers in the humanities and social sciences are thrilled to hear geneticists publicly state that races don't exist. When geneticists advance this idea, they mean that we cannot infer social characteristics from genetic variations among individuals or groups. But at the same time that the social sciences' desire to prevent physiological analysis from interfering with this field of study appears to have been satisfied, biologists have begun to decipher the codes that will allow for a better understanding of the biochemical mechanisms through which the intergenerational transmission of physiological traits occurs. In other words, the constructivist paradigm is occupying the entire intellectual space of the social sciences at the same moment that, for the first time in the history of humanity, the biological sciences have become capable of precisely describing the causalities linked to heredity.[7]

Despite the sense that a global approach to racial questions is pertinent to research (and to public policies), any analysis of these issues conducted in the humanities and social sciences is by definition situated within a specific historical and cultural context. Race isn't written about in France or Germany in the same way that it is in Great Britain or, even less so, in the United States or Latin America. Our countries' respective histories bequeathed legacies that diverge dramatically on the elements essential to understanding racial policies. European countries continue to digest the very long-term consequences of two historical upheavals: first, the suicide of Europe during the two World Wars, and more specifically the human, material, and moral destruction caused by Nazism; and second, the pendular movement from colonization to decolonization, and then to the migration toward Europe of populations that more or less inherited the colonial situations created by Europeans in the migrants' home countries. The United States and many Latin American countries must, for their part, bear responsibility for the dual legacies of the genocide of Native Americans and the chattel slavery endured by Native American populations and masses of deported Africans. These two sets of experiences have generated different ways of reflecting on the processes of racial segregation and persecution. On the one hand, it is necessary to read the works of researchers of both worlds while taking into account their roots in different historical trajectories. On the other hand, it is important not to act as if

European societies and American societies have lived in separate universes: connections and reciprocal influences have never ceased, including in the field of racial discrimination.

The way the humanities and social sciences approach the subject of race in Western Europe in general, and in quite a unique way in France, is certainly different from what can be observed in the United States. This divergence begins with vocabulary. In contemporary French, the term "race" has completely disappeared from the scholarly lexicon. This can be explained by the fact that its meaning was radically restricted after 1945. Indeed, whenever "race" has been mentioned in France, following the end of World War II, it has been solely to designate the biological unit of a population. Restricted to that sense, the term can therefore no longer be mobilized to designate a people, culture, nation, or any other descriptor used to define populations by their cultural, social, or political characteristics. In truth, the term arouses such repugnance among researchers that it is also no longer used to designate biologically similar populations. It is as if, in reality, it has become impossible in France to strip the word "race" of its political connotations and the memory of the crimes committed in its name. The phenomenon of a stigmatized group appropriating a stigma is absent: racialized groups only recently adopted the term "race" to use against their persecutors. The activist circles that have begun to deploy that lexical strategy are the same as those that adhere to a so-called decolonial ideology, which is expressed as an anti–white supremacy discourse, if not as black supremacy. Both, white and black, refer less to skin color than to a political separation between Europeans and second- and third-generation migrants, whose origins are the former imperial colonies of the French Republic. In such a political context, French scholars have to make decisions about the notions they introduce in their analyses and surveys. "Racism" is unendingly used to designate various forms of collective discrimination. But at the same time, the term "race," which should be the referent on which political racism is based, in fact remains absent from racist discourse itself.

The widespread idea that in France public statistics would not produce data on the nationalities and geographical origins of naturalized persons is simply false.[8] For example, as the great TeO (Trajectories and Origins) survey—carried out by two major public research institutions in demography and statistics—shows, it is possible to produce quantitative data on ethnic discrimination in France, even though the administration does not recognize the validity of ethnoracial categories in the population census.[9] The recently published results of this survey confirm the fact that starting with equal training, the careers of postcolonial migrants and their descendants are hardly successful, and these citizens suffer from discrimination, for example in housing. Similarly, the French government has annual statistics on racist offenses and crimes.[10] One can draw two conclusions: racial discrimination does exist in France, and the idea that color blindness dominates in the country is simply wrong.

For a European reader, what strikes in the mass of American historiographic production is, first of all, the overwhelming domination of a certain chronology. Indeed, the great majority of the works propose an equivalence between the practice of mass slavery and the development of a racist social system. Now, as the massive use of slavery began in the English colonies during the last third of the seventeenth century, it follows that the history of race is concentrated on the period that begins in 1660 and continues until the 1960s. And within this chronology, the most recent periods are incomparably more studied than the oldest. When one reads this scholarship in Europe, this way of cutting history appears purely Anglocentric and calls for at least two criticisms. The first relates to the slave trade, a system that, in the Iberian monarchies, dates back to a period long before the *Mayflower* left the quays of Plymouth. The second criticism concerns the exclusive relation between racism and slavery that European experiences of racial discrimination, unrelated to slavery, contradict. The histories were different, and the narratives diverge. One of the main questions this book addresses, then, is this: how can the construction of the problem of race by a historiography born of European experience dialogue with the humanities and social sciences that are produced in the United States?

Definitions

To progress in the argument, a series of definitions of race and racism that are developed throughout this book will guide the reader:

1. Racial prejudice or racism postulates that social and moral (or cultural, religious, political, etc.) characteristics of people and groups are transmitted from generation to generation through vectors found in bodily tissue and fluids (blood, sperm, milk); when the relevant conditions are met on the ideological, normative, and political levels, then fluids like blood, sperm, and milk must be understood by the historian not as symbols, images, or metaphors, but as material objects in themselves. If a historical source uses blood merely as a kind of metaphorical expression of a spiritual principle or social process, it is not proposing a racial definition of identity (or alterity, which amounts to the same thing);

2. Racial discrimination, or racism, is based on the notion that a minority cannot join the social majority to which it aspires to belong regardless of the political circum-

stances present and regardless of voluntary individual efforts to reduce the distance separating it from the social majority to which it aspires to belong; an unalterable element remains, which renders the aspiration to rejoin the social majority either futile or impossible. The host of this immutable remainder, real or metaphysical, is the person's body. This incapacity to change or rid oneself of a heritage (or heredity) affects all the individuals who belong to a stigmatized group equally;

3. Racist policies aim, primarily, to impede the processes by which marginal or stigmatized populations can integrate a shared political space within the society in which they reside. In other words, when the members of a family or group undergo a process of social and political transformation that will result in reducing the distance separating them from the majority society, then racists will identify the minorities' differences as physically rooted, indelible, and present in all individuals of said family or group without exception, and this denunciation is motivated by the desire to slow the process of integration. Racists will declare that the alterity embedded in the body of the other is inalterable, because its roots run deeper than all social affiliation, and so, they will denounce the idea of a shared affiliation or belonging or the disappearance of differences, declaring this idea to be a dangerous illusion.

If we accept this three-tiered definition, racism does not consist of defining alterity, or otherness, as a static and visible reality, and rejecting those that fall into this group, namely because that is the definition of any form of xenophobia. Racism, which should be understood as a narrower political phenomenon, is a plan of action consisting of producing alterity in a society in order to feed mechanisms of stigmatization, distinction, and discrimination. Historical research on the formation of racial categories thus confronts both methodological and theoretical uncertainties. Making a number of those difficulties explicit remains the best way to illustrate where we currently stand on these questions.

CHAPTER ONE

A Challenge for the Humanities and Social Sciences

Questions of Method

Conducting research on the theme of race within the social sciences consists of identifying a specifically racial core among the assortment of prejudices, phobias, political programs, and norms that we vaguely qualify as racist. This book addresses the specific role that historians can play in interdisciplinary discussion of those phenomena. Through it, I hope to spark reactions and prompt discussion of not only the historical dimension of the problem of race, but also its sociological, anthropological, and philosophical dimensions. This work is therefore aimed at identifying the ways historical research can elucidate the study of the formation of racial categories as political tools and resources in human societies. To that end, my historical analysis has two objectives:

1. To propose a chronology of the formation of racial categories in the West that is therefore not limited to the
nineteenth and twentieth centuries. Some historians
reconstruct documented ways of thinking and understanding from much earlier periods, such as, for example, classic antiquity. Texts (and images) conserved from
that period reveal how heredity or climatic variations
were understood.[1] Their distant legacies transformed
authors like Hippocrates and Galen into incontestable
authorities on subjects like the congenital formation
of individuals and the influence of food or climate on
a person's disposition. For centuries, theories about the
balance of the four elements (air, fire, water, earth) or
the influence of humors on personality served as the
foundation for the practice of medicine, as well as the
psychological description of individuals. In parallel,
thanks to geographers like Herodotus, Pliny, or Ptolemy,
the idea that societies were divided into differentiable
natural and social groups persisted for an equally long
period of time.[2] Finally, texts by Aristotle include lines
of reasoning that can be used to explain the distinction
between masters and slaves by the latter's natural inferiority.[3] During the European Middle Ages, the Renaissance, and the Enlightenment, European societies and
the colonies in their empires were host to phenomena
of relegation, discrimination, persecution, and, at times,
extermination. These efforts to repress or eradicate were
often justified politically by racial notions of alterity. The
historian's task thus consists of making choices, based
on our knowledge of past societies, in order to answer
the question: When? Or more precisely, at what moment
did racial policies appear in the history of those societies? The answers to that question can orient all attempts

made by the social sciences to identify and understand racial and racist phenomena.

2. To prepare scholars within the humanities and social sciences, students, and citizens to confront any challenges that may be created by the currently unpredictable outcomes of research in the field of genetic biology. It is, of course, indispensable to continue to denounce the ideological agenda and racist policies espoused by sociobiology.[4] However, we must acknowledge that as the humanities and social sciences continue to develop their respective expertise, it is critical to monitor what genetic biology may contribute in the future to our understanding of man's development in society.

⟨⸙⸙⸙⸙⸙⟩

Racial thinking and racial politics do not have the sole purpose of giving form and legitimacy to social domination. In the long history of the shaping of Western societies, the certainty that the qualities and abilities of people in intergenerational succession are transmitted through the vector of the body was first used to ensure the sustainability of privileges in the noble families. So, the racial argument was mobilized just as much to justify the election of the best as to explain the stigmatization of the supposedly bad. To use the phrase of Charles de Miramon, "medieval society represents itself as a meritocracy of the virtuous men even though social reproduction is based on heredity."[5] Of course, election and stigma are built to mirror one another. The superior qualities are transmitted through the same channels as the lower ones, starting with the blood. For centuries people attributed the ability to convey the moral and social character of people to that precious liquid. In some cases of extreme enforcement of racism in modern times, blood has not been considered a metaphor. This can be seen in the ban on "real" Germans accepting blood transfusions from Jews at the beginning of the Third Reich, or in the refusal of the US Red Cross to accept black blood donors during World War II.[6] Early modern historians do not agree on one point: whether the faculty that people have attributed to the blood should be understood as a symbol or as actual power transmitted in a material way. The social efficiency of lineage transmission, for better or for worse, indicates that the power of the blood was not understood to be metaphorical.

Scholars who research racial segregation have welcomed the distinction between rules and practices. Indeed, many investigations of past or present societies show that the rules governing segregation based on race apply more or less radically in practice. When studying how identity is assigned by contemporary bureaucracies, we find, just as we do in the self-definition games that people play themselves, that people can change their identity during their lifetimes. The "passing" processes offer a large array of cases. This observation invites us to not take quite literally the racial rules, and to not see them as the perfect transcript of social life. As part of historical research, the chronological depth and knowledge of lineages through genealogical investigation may lead to the same skepticism. One can demonstrate that many families have gradually escaped the racial fate the rules defined for them. Showing that the rules of social exclusion based on the familial origin of individuals could be circumvented in a certain number of cases allows us to moderate the critical view that we can take of the societies of the past, or it allows us to distinguish different systems of segregation according to their degree of intransigence. However, two objections may be raised to such an approach. On the one hand, the confrontation between rules and practices is an issue whose conclusion is always given in advance: the practices depart from the rules. People do not behave like legal subjects on whom the law and norms impose requirements and prohibitions. This discrepancy is found in any place and at any time. It therefore demonstrates nothing specific. In contrast, under the gaze of the social sciences, configurations in which the behavior of actors incorporate a number of more or less formal norms remain specific, and the resulting practices of racial identification are shaped by the reality of social life. Another point though is that the fact that some individuals belonging to stigmatized groups knew how to escape the stigma does not prove that the stigma procedures are ineffective.

The case of segregation in the United States provides a historical example of this phenomenon. The principle of the one-drop rule—the rule of hypodescendance—defines the "wrong" origin and specifies this origin down even to a single trace of what determines the character of the individual. In the US South, segregating public spaces and banning mixed marriages were maneuvers to deprive African American citizens of their right to vote. In the same society the phenomenon of "passing"— the implementation of a personal program by which an individual whose origin was partly African could pass for "white"— was of great importance. The argument that practices differ from rules would help here to explain the flaw in the argument that because of the many cases of passing the general system was not really racist. The attention to social configurations that gave rise to the phenomenon of passing highlights all the resources people mobilized to escape their condition. Thus, the possibility of getting rid of the stigma does not reveal the fragility of the stigma, but rather its strength.

Looking at earlier periods, stepping back further, the argument that rules equal practices seems even weaker. Indeed, historically, when people have analyzed genealogies of many generations, the probability of detecting a "racially suspect" individual in the lineage has increased. In sixteenth-century

Spain, the repressive authority of the Inquisition rested exactly on this probability, as when the tribunal showed its ability to identify the presence of a suspicious origin in one sixty-fourth of the blood of an individual. Historians should not draw from the high probability that no one escapes the presence of an infamous ancestry the conclusion that the rules of exclusion of suspects were little or poorly enforced. If an individual can escape his or her racial condition during his or her lifetime, or if his or her family can do so after several generations, historians must take into account that social and legal processes involved in both cases may not be exactly the same. To erase a stigmatized racial condition in few years, or in a few decades or generations, is a very different experience for the different individuals concerned. Depending on how long it takes to improve one's own condition, the same amount of movement can be seen as a failure or as a success. Historians should pay more attention to how heavily time weighs on individual human experience.

The rules/practices opposition thus supplies the conclusions of an investigation before it has even begun. But what colonial experiences and racist societies teach us is that personal mobility, driven by a desire to change status, doesn't reveal the inefficacity of racial categories, but the importance that individuals attach to the possibility of escaping them. In other words, a society that imagines itself as a society of mixture, a society of the melting pot, a society in which certain individuals and families may change their racial identity, may at the same time be a society in which racial barriers can deeply segment people, either formally or informally.

Taking a long-term historical view of concepts of race and racism doesn't hurt our ability to assess more recent history.

Rather, any historian, whatever the period of study, addresses racial issues keeping in mind, more or less consciously, the triad composed of the Jim Crow laws in the United States, Nazism in Europe, and apartheid in South Africa. These are common points of reference to all researchers working on these problems, whether they recognize these points of references explicitly, or these points of references remain implicit or even unconscious. Therefore, according to a good historical method, the historian must be careful to avoid seeing this triad as the inevitable culmination of a long history, and trying to trace this outcome back to its origins. It's necessary, instead, to acknowledge awareness of the triad as the starting point of any critical approach to the historical legacy of racism—that is to say, it is a defining feature of the political and intellectual situation—in which researchers today find themselves when they consider working on these issues. Since historians of all periods explicitly or implicitly compare their research field with the contemporary triad, in order to show that their cases are similar or, conversely, to show that they differ, they should know the background of how these contemporary racist policies were implemented and developed. Therefore, historians who work on racial issues should be specialists in the period of their specialty, and at the same time, they should be well informed about the history of Jim Crow, Nazism, and apartheid. Again, this is not always the case.

In histories that deal with hierarchy in past societies, the dominant trend is to reject the idea that social classes had a racial dimension before the establishment of racist regimes. This position is based on the rejection of Nazism as reference point or lens through which to see past societies. It promotes the good sense of rejecting *reductio ad Hitlerum* in Leo Strauss's words, or as we say now, Godwin's law. But fairly often a misunderstanding of Hitler's regime undermines this argument.

We find, for example, from the pen of Anglo historians the idea that under the Ancien Régime in Europe and in the colonies, race was not a matter of biology but of lineage, and some historians see this as a major difference between past societies and more recent, post-Hitler societies, which supposedly define race according to biological or genetic criteria. However, a careful reading of the 1935 Nuremberg Laws on the Protection of German Blood shows that the identification of the Jewish nature of individuals relies on lineage. Indeed, clearing the stain in a mixed Jewish genealogy is possible only if the grandparent "Jew" was never affiliated with a synagogue. The officials and leaders of the Nazi party had come to the conclusion that the laws of the botanist Gregor Mendel on the transmission of hereditary traits could not help determine whether a "mestizo" half Jew could join the German people and the German citizenship, or whether he or she would be excluded forever. Only a "review of the history of his family and his political positions in general" could provide a citizen under scrutiny the possibility of being cleared, on a case by case basis. In contrast, German Jews who participated in Jewish life, worshiped in a synagogue, were members of Jewish associations, and preferred intramarriage were of course excluded from the German people. This shows that the Nazis, despite their dissemination of wild ideas that borrowed notions from the observation of hereditary transmissions, targeted their victims based on religious, cultural, and political criteria and on lineage. In the end, race was about lineage for the Nazis too! From this point of view, Nazi anti-Semitism is racism without race, if we are using a genetic understanding of race.

The scientific tools and racial engineering the Nazis mobilized in the service of extermination are in no way an indicator that their interpretation of the world and their racial agenda rested on a scientific or biological foundation. That is a faulty political analysis. Industrial technologies of death were not backed by the science of life. As we know, the discoveries that made it possible to map the human genome were published after the collapse of the Nazi regime, and the Nazis never could have defined "Jewishness" genetically. So we cannot under any circumstances use the Nazi case as a touchstone for distinguishing a "protoracism" of the early modern era from genuine scientific or genetic racism in the contemporary age. Conversely, according to anthropologist Nancy Farriss, "Physical anthropologists tell us that scientifically speaking there is no such thing as race. But for most of recorded history, we must deal with people unaware of this recent finding and for whom race was a palpable reality."[7] There is no reason to assume that the people in earlier periods had acquired, like us, the persuasion that it was absurd to divide (or describe) societies along racial categories. So, we cannot say that earlier societies did not divide people according to some notion of inherited race and that the Nazis were the first to enforce radical racism, using modern science to justify discrimination and extermination. Upon closer examination both parts of this argument fall apart.

What makes Nazi racial policy (or Jim Crow laws or South African apartheid) different from the oldest forms of discrimination is not the blooming of any scientific revolution but rather, that it is the consequence of democratic and liberal revolutions, which gave rise to sovereign nation states, setting the stage for national citizenship, and the triumph of nationalist ideology (there is only one version of nationalist ideology, and it is always dangerous). It is important to remember that racial reasoning was enriched, during a long nineteenth century, with arguments that owed nothing to the development of observation of the mechanisms of heredity. One such argument was that language plays a natural role in the formation of the character of a people. Another phenomenon that bolstered racial reasoning was the historical and philological forgery that tried to prove that Western people, languages, culture, and civilization are of Indo-Europeans descent.[8] Another such phenomenon was the romantic enthronement of the art of barbaric people as opposed to a Jewish failure to achieve it.[9] One last example is the rhetorical justifications of colonial enterprises, which were based, as during the Ancien Régime, on arguments about the development of civilization in an evolutionary framework, although such arguments did not include genetic concepts, even when it came to excluding mestizo citizens in the colonial dominions. The history of the world through its races that Gobineau lays out in *An Essay on the Inequality of the Human Races* (1853) is a lament for the destruction of the aristocratic principle and has little to do with the medical knowledge of his time. Of course, the eugenic programs of nineteenth and twentieth centuries forged an imaginary of heredity and put on the white coat of the laboratory, but even these programs were pseudoscientific at best. In other words, modern racism is modern in a political sense, because nationalism charged it with new energy. But it is not supported by scientific modernity. In the end it makes little sense to split "protoracism" of the Ancien Régime and deem it archaic, to say it is ultimately less scientific than modern racism.

It was not scientific development but, it seems, the creation of a national state and the abolition of slavery that heavily shaped racial policies in the nineteenth and twentieth centuries. If that is the case, then we should indeed focus our attention on political history and social history in order to understand the evolution of those racial policies, rather than looking to the history of science. That said, the latter field remains extremely valuable when it comes to clearly identifying the ideas and conclusions borrowed by those who endorsed racial policies, most often indiscriminately, to confer a "precise" dimension to their social engineering. This is especially the case because the first probabilistic hypotheses about heredity were not the first resources to be borrowed from the natural sciences to support racist arguments. Far from it, they were predated by much older static classifications of human beings, based on the Linnaean model, as well as later dynamic classifications. Medical beliefs about the structure of humors in the body and the virtues or vices transported by blood are older still, and they too were used to classify people and divide the population into distinct groups. However, despite the fact that scientific tools have long been used to further racist ideologies, and that these tools are worthy of in-depth study, they do not explain the origins of racist thought, and other types of historical inquiry are crucial for understanding race and racism in the West.

What to Do with the Word "Race"?

A clarification regarding the current debate on the use of the word "race" in French social sciences and public policy is called for. On March 11, 2012, François Hollande, then a presidential candidate, declared that "the [French] Republic does not fear diversity because diversity is movement, it's life. There is no diversity of races. There is no room in the Republic for race. And so, after the presidential election, I will ask parliament to remove the word 'race' from our constitution."[10] Indeed, the first article of the French Constitution reads: "France shall be an indivisible, secular, democratic and social Republic. It shall ensure the equality of all citizens before the law, without distinction of origin, race or religion. It shall respect all beliefs." In the particularly dramatic climate surrounding the electoral campaign, Nicolas Sarkozy, the incumbent president vying for reelection, reacted to his opponent's proposition by stating: "The word 'race' is in the preamble to the 1946 Constitution, which is a sacred text, written by the Resistance fighters, the people who after the war said: 'Never again do we want racism.' On the day that we erase the word 'racism,' will we have erased the idea? Come on, it's absurd! . . . The problem isn't the word, the problem is reality."[11]

This political sparring, and the subsequent measures taken, are symptomatic, at least from the perspective that concerns us. They reenact a debate that took place in the early 1990s, under pressure from a group of lawyers who formed the Charte Galilée 1990 collective, and which prompted a large conference in the French Senate in 1992. At that time, voices as disparate as those of Chantal Millon-Delsol and Étienne Balibar protested that removing the term "race" would not only do little to bolster the fight against racism but would in fact create the illusion that it had been won. Millon-Delsol went on the offensive, foreshadowing Nicolas Sarkozy's later arguments:

> The question is: will removing the word "race" make it easier to dethrone its underlying ideology? It seems to me that the best strategy is confrontation: a harmful sociological and ideological reality can be deployed under shadow of indifference or forgetting, which can lead us to believe that it is not part of the social norm. The only way to combat this is if a society designates this toxic reality permanently to affirm it has subsumed it and, in this case, is dedicated to destroying it.[12]

Balibar believed that attempts to remove the term "race" from the French Constitution reflected a political desire to break the continuum between discrimination based on the racial definition of alterities and discriminations stemming from other sources (religion, migrant status, social or territorial relegation, etc.) Consequently, he emphasized the need for a disconnect between the history of racial policies and that of biological sciences, which is an essential topic within historiography that was addressed in the introduction of this work:

> For the word *race* . . . does not *intrinsically* have a "biological" signification. That meaning is, strictly speaking, a "secondary elaboration." The word's primary meaning is *historical and social.* It goes hand in hand with the imaginary representation of the hereditary substance and genealogical structure of social groups (which in the modern era are more and more often national groups, actual or potential "majorities," or "national minorities"), and with the projection of social differences in an imaginary world of somatic markers (skin color, conformation of traits and members, etc.). The idea that *race* . . . could have a "biological" signification is a historical hoax. The term *race* in its modern, discriminatory usage acquired its function and value *before* any "biological" elaboration, and it is likely to maintain them *beyond* said elaboration.[13]

The above examples are belated French manifestations of a debate launched much earlier in the United States, where the process of eliminating the word "race" from the lexicons of both the social sciences and public policy began in the early 1950s. In America, the desire to erase the term "race" from academic and everyday vocabulary dates at least as far back as anthropologist Ashley Montagu's vain crusade. He wrote:

> It may be difficult for those who believe in what I. A. Richards has called "The Divine Right of Words" to accept the suggestion that a word such as "race," which has exercised so evil a tyranny over the minds of men, should be permanently dethroned from the vocabulary, but that constitutes

all the more reason for trying, remembering that the meaning of a word is the action it produces.[14]

His quest would end bitterly as the word "race" was never
banned from Anglophone publications related to the social
sciences or biology.

More than a mere question of lexical preference, the French
use of the word "race" must be understood within the context
of a virulent debate that pits those who support the establishment of statistics that describe populations according to ethnic
origin or the nationality of their ancestors against those who
oppose such statistics.[15] Those who resist any analysis based
on racial distinctions see race as a handicap to social scientific
research. However, it is more productive to see the question of
"race" as one of many problematics that should be approached
as, itself, the object of investigation. This approach neither
accepts existing racial designations nor rejects any analysis of
racial categories out of hand but rather involves a deeper study
of the practices of racialization that exist in a given society. As
Didier Fassin writes,

> Discomfort, both ethical and practical, with designating
> the realities of the issue of race is not an obstacle to under-
> standing these realities but rather the prerequisite. Our
> inability to name implies an obligation to think. Consider
> the substance of racial categories and racist policies, which
> nowadays don't always appear as such and which must be
> exhumed from the actions and discourse that cover and
> conceal them.[16]

The proposed method formulated by Fassin within the context of a sociological study on contemporary France can be useful to historians of earlier periods and other regions. Indeed, if
it is reasonable to study racialization practices and discourses

in a society that tends to exclude raciological lexicon from institutional language, for example public policies, then the absence of this same lexicon in earlier eras cannot be cited as proof that racial categories had not yet been formed. If racism can exist today in the absence of racial language, policies of racial discrimination may well have existed in the past in the absence of words that would have attested to their racist nature.

Racial Ideologies and Their Contradictions

The analytical framework of this book is based on an understanding of race according to neither socioeconomic domination—its extreme manifestation being the slave trade and chattel slavery—nor physical appearance—the most obvious model being skin color. In no way does that signify underestimating the mass crimes of chattel slavery, Jim Crow laws, and apartheid practices, which, along with the Nazi political and legal regime, share the distinction as the most radically racist and deadly policies in the contemporary Western world. But in the United States, the most natural approach to the question of racial discrimination is centered precisely on color and slavery. The current and historical reasons for that orientation of American research are both self-evident and legitimate. Nevertheless, it is necessary for scholars in the United States to move beyond that framework and grasp the longer history of race and racism, in which it is clear that race is a political construction and not merely a system of segregation and persecution based on phenotypical characteristics, such as skin color.

In that context, the historiographical debate around slavery has been split between two explanatory models for the dehumanization, cruelty, and enormity of the slave trade.[17] Some historians argue that the implementation of that system was made possible by a long, preexisting history of stigmatization and suspicion of African populations in Renaissance-era Europe.[18] Others believe that the modes of production that relied on the large-scale exploitation of slaves kindled a discourse that justified that abomination by the natural inferiority of its victims.[19] The current and historical reasons why American research is focused on the long-term effects of the slave trade are, again, both obvious and legitimate. The aim of translating this book into English is to offer the reader a point of view that differs from the dominant tone on the above themes, which leans heavily on ideas of scientific production in both cases. While I plan to break with this tradition, I nonetheless aim to continue dialogue with scholars in the United States.

The title of this book, *Race Is about Politics: Lessons from History*, indicates my intention—that is, to identify how the work of historians can facilitate specific understandings within the much larger field of human and social sciences. In Europe, as well as in the United States, sociology, ethnology, political science, philosophy, and art criticism contribute, alongside history, to our understanding of phenomena of racialization, racist behavior, and the expression and diffusion of racial prejudices. The thesis outlined in the following pages consists of showing that the methodological choice of chronological depth in the study of race and racism allows scholars in all fields to gain a new understanding and to approach the subject from specific analytical angles that are not offered by other disciplines within the human and social sciences. The proposals formulated in this work are in large part the result of the persistent cohesion of the human sciences (including the literary domain) and the social sciences in France. That cohesion represents a clear divergence from the division of disciplines in the United States.

Once we accept the usefulness of a historical approach to the study of race, it is important to define the lens through which historians should look in order to more accurately and fruitfully offer a narrative of the formation of racial categories. If we consider that racial distinction is a political tool and resource available in a given society, then we are dealing with an ideology. This means something much more substantial and articulated than a simple series of stereotypes. Historians work to establish inventories of various kinds of representations of cultural alterity, in different time periods and locations, to the extent that sources allow. The historical creation of images of the Other can be traced from the portrayal of prisoners with "negroid" features in Egyptian bas-reliefs to the poster for Veit Arlan's *Jud Süß*, among countless other examples. These artifacts usually have a double, indissociable aim: to note a difference and to create a distinction. If we were to focus our analysis on the contents of those stereotypes, we would be prevented from understanding the process of distinction itself. When inventories were created, they most often produced tautologies for Europeans in the vein of "the African is inferior because he is described as an ape-like being" or "the Jew arouses disgust because he is depicted as repugnant." The information gained through this kind of study is quickly exhausted. On the contrary, an approach in terms of ideology, because it is far more demanding, offers entirely different perspectives. It entails, in the manner of Giuliano Gliozzi,[20] understanding altogether, as a whole, the socioeconomic system and the politico-institutional and normative framework of a given society, as well as the registers of expression and interpretation of the world that produce and give meaning to manifestations of hostility and to the desire to relegate stigmatized populations. By using this kind of analysis, we can identify the links between racial discourse, the rules that frame politics and policies, and the agency of individuals and groups, including of course the victims of stigmatization.

Nothing allows us to better grasp the difference between seeing race through the lens of a series of distrustful stereotypes or attitudes and developing an understanding of an entire race-based ideology than considering "colonial situations," to borrow Georges Balandier's expression.[21] The creation of colonial societies relies on three factors: (1) the substitution of local political authorities by foreign or local agents who report to political institutions in the colonizing country; (2) the settlement of new residents from the colonizing region and the appropriation of economic resources, beginning with the best land, to the colonists' benefit; (3) the production of a legitimizing discourse, or a doctrine, in other words, that gives meaning to the phenomenon and accompanies its evolution. When historians recount the stages of the creation of colonial racial ideologies, they analyze the social, political, and cultural processes that define the rules of hierarchization in social relations, as they are understood and integrated by both the dominant and dominated groups. Such studies have been conducted on a wide variety of settings, from England's diminishment of Irish society's autonomy beginning in the central Middle Ages,[22] to Frantz Fanon's and Albert Memmi's revelations of the trap enclosing both colonizers and colonized in a no-win confrontation,[23] and including the definition of a space specific to the Spanish monarchy's Native American subjects, as documented by the vast manuscript compiled by the Peruvian nobleman Felipe Guamán Poma de Ayala, at the end of the sixteenth century and the beginning of the seventeenth century.[24] The colonial, and now postcolonial, question should be of primary importance in any historical study of racial ideology.

{≈≈≈≈◖≋◗≈≈≈≈}

The hypothesis of the fixity of human conditions assumes that no social or historical accident of nature is able to modify individuals or populations. That notion can easily feed off a polygenist perspective of the history of mankind, meaning the idea that several distinct species of human beings coexist on Earth. It is particularly suited to supporting a political project aimed at keeping apparently different populations separate. Polygenism thus appears to be the perfect theory for any ideology that confines individuals and communities to a form of unalterable natural identity. It is the theory most apt to justify segregation, hierarchization, and even slavery. In contrast, monogenism doesn't diverge from the biblical narrative that considers all humanity to have one shared origin. This interpretive framework is, hypothetically, the most apt to foster universalistic, relativistic, and evolutionist structures. In reality, as shown by Silvia Sebastiani's work, the distribution of roles between polygenism and monogenism isn't that simple, in particular if we examine their respective contributions to the development of a racial conception of the diversity of man.[25]

Efforts to organize and classify nature, undertaken by figures ranging from Linnaeus to Buffon and from Lamarck to Darwin, or in other words from the fixity of creation to evolutionary theory, produced an entire scientific vocabulary, in terms of kingdoms, classes, genus, species, and so on.[26] Beginning with the Age of Enlightenment, and throughout the nineteenth century, natural history served as a foundation on which to construct explanations for the physiological and civilizational diversity of the world's societies. But, depending on which nomenclatures were used—those based on the hypothesis of the fixity of species, or those, on the contrary, based on the theory of evolution—the impact of natural history models on the social sciences has varied greatly.

As a result, the intellectual discussion that emerged between those two positions, starting with Linnaeus's *Systema Naturae*, fueled the ambivalence of racial thinking about humankind, caught between the hypothesis of fixity and the obsessive fear of a degeneration produced by interracial marriage and the resulting offspring.[27] Societies on the American continent during the second half of the nineteenth century and the first half of the twentieth century reveal the complete range of that spectrum of possibility: laws against all interracial marriage in the United States, on the one hand, and large campaigns in several Latin American countries aimed at attracting European migrants toward the goal of "improving the race" by "whitening" it, on the other.[28] In the former case, segregation was intended to prevent the "black element" from affecting the composition of white families; in the latter, the call for contributions of white blood was aimed at reducing Native American and African dominance in societies in which Europeans had universally been the minority since the conquest of the Americas.

Racial thought was therefore unable to choose between the fixist argument, that races are static features of groups of people and cannot be changed, and the more dynamic one, no less racist, that races can improve or degenerate. Thus both relegation and stigmatization stemmed from the idea that accidents of nature can negatively modify a person's essence. This single underlying idea is a generic belief that, beginning in the mid-nineteenth century, scientific debate referred to as the "heritability of acquired characteristics," but it is in fact much older. The notion of congenital inferiority and the natural transmission of the condition of slavery, for example, fall under this category. Finally, the hypothesis of the historic mutation of a people, in the sense of its inferiorization, was also conceivable: it was applied, for example, to the Jews (or Israelites), whose nature was said to have transformed after they refused to join the alliance sealed with the death and resurrection of Jesus Christ.[29] Because of their blindness, the Jews were believed to have gone from the highest rank of humanity to the most contemptible.

The contradiction between fixity and metamorphosis manifests in a multitude of ways. The aristocracy, for example, viewed nobility as a fixed condition. Yet royal ideology dictated that certain types of activities were ennobling. Belonging to a good lineage and performing the right duties were conditions that validated each other, and this mutually reinforced relationship was protected and heightened by a congenital transmission of virtues and a guarantee of recognition by the royal institution. However, theories about nobility inevitably confront the mystery of noble accession, namely the unsolvable question: when someone is formally granted nobility by order of the king, wasn't he or she already noble before being recognized as such? Royal grace was the agent of a mutation, a change of nature—a miracle, in other words. In this case, it is clear how three, somewhat contradictory, mechanisms contributed to forging the ideology of the dominant nobility: the perpetuity of lineage, the exercise of functions and activities that attest to the noble condition, and the almost thaumaturgical act of a king in "creating" nobles. Ultimately, the natural fixity of conditions, the heritability of acquired characteristics, and the belief in the effects of mutation combined easily within the political ideologies of the early modern era.

Fixity or immutability thus has two faces. On the positive side, it is the faculty of the good part of humanity to perpetuate its qualities, its ways of being; in the negative is the capacity of the evil part of humanity to persevere in its errors, in its moral ugliness. Racism reproaches those whom it identifies as the unhealthy part of society because they cannot correct their unacceptable propensities. Paradoxically, this argument is all the more virulent as racists, in fact, react precisely against the ability of groups qualified as foreigners or unhealthy or evil to join the common life of the majority of society. That is why the

question of fixity and mutation have such an important place
in the history of racial politics.

{≈≈≈≈≈}

The study of Christian societies at the end of the Middle Ages
and during the Early Modern era raises the issue of the incompatibility between, on the one hand, Saint Paul's message
("There is neither Jew nor Gentile, neither slave nor free, nor
is there male and female, for you are all one in Christ Jesus,"
Galatians 3:28) and the efficacy of grace ("If you belong to
Christ, then you are Abraham's seed, and heirs according to
the promise," Galatians 3:29); and, on the other hand, rules
of segregation based on an individual or a people's natural inferiority and inability to change. For example, persecution of
the descendants of converts in Iberian societies at the end of
the Middle Ages and during the Ancien Régime was a rejection
of the former principles. By decreeing that the descendants of
converted Jews or Muslims remained suspect and undoubtedly harbored threats to society, Iberian courts and rules of
blood purity denied the efficacy of baptism,[30] as if the water of
that sacrament was unable to wash away blood of bad origin.
The case of converted Jews on the Iberian Peninsula can be
viewed in many ways as the oldest foundation of modern racism. By the end of the Middle Ages, the Jewish community in
Spain and Portugal was by far the largest in Europe and even
the Mediterranean basin. But coexistence with the Christian
majority in both urban and rural zones had created a situation
in which, outside of the rituals of religious life, it had become
difficult to distinguish, at first glance, a Jew from a Christian.
Beginning in the thirteenth century (Fourth Lateran Council,
1215), an obsessive fear of sexual relations between Jews and
Christians resulted in Jews being forced to wear a distinctive

clothing marker,[31] a sign, if proof was needed, of Jews' invisibility, because it was only with a marker that they could be told apart.

But the feeling that the intermingling of Jews and Christians represented a spiritual and social danger intensified when Jews converted en masse, either voluntarily or under duress, notably after a series of extremely violent pogroms (1391–92).[32] From that point on, Jews (who were no longer Jews) became twice as invisible. The same issue arose, albeit in a different way, for the Moriscos, the Muslim minority forced to convert.[33] The dissolution of religious diversity takes the form of a uniformity of behavior, clothing, and habits. It is more the case of the former Jews than Muslims forcibly converted, for many of the former have long preserved particular practices and a language. But in both cases, the process consisted of reducing the whole of society to the Christian church alone. But at the heart of this communion, in fact, the old differences persisted in the eyes of many "old Christians." But since difference was no longer based on identifiable forms, behaviors, or habits, the persistent difference had to lie in what is not seen: that is, the nature of the blood flowing in the veins of these people. Hence the proliferation of the idea that their bad origin was transmitted, social appearances notwithstanding, by an intrinsic nature whose vector was blood. Here, we can observe the model for the process of "alteration" by which racial thought transforms the same into the other, as Claude-Olivier Doron precisely and exhaustively shows in his recently published book.[34] This foundation can be found at the core of the political tool kit used by Spanish and Portuguese conquistadors in the construction of their transcontinental empires. They came to Africa, Asia, and then America, having lived, if only as witnesses, with the tensions that resulted from the segregation of the descendants of the converts. That is to say, they conceived of conquest as a process that could bring immense benefits but could also alter the nature of the conquerors because of their contacts with populations of a different nature.

The antinomy between the universalist view of redemption for the whole of humankind and racism is not unique to Christianity. Islam is riddled by an equally powerful, and indeed not so different, contradiction. Studies of medieval theological and legal corpuses have even shown that the earliest version of the myth of Ham, used to justify the enslavement of black men, was created by medieval Islamic societies.[35] This myth borrows from an episode from Genesis in which Ham is the only of Noah's three sons to see his inebriated father naked. When he woke, Noah is said to have condemned Ham and his descendants to perpetual servitude. Some exegetes of the Old Testament interpreted that curse as directed against black-skinned men. This version of the story is nearly absent from medieval rabbinical tradition.[36] In contrast, it occupies a significant place in part of Islamic tradition in the earliest centuries. The Islamic practice of slave raids on sub-Saharan populations and the presence of slave markets in Muslim Spain predate similar practices by Christians and are two legacies Christian Europe received from Mediterranean Islam. During the Middle Ages, several European languages abandoned the Latin term *servus* in favor of the word "slave." That shift reflected the existence of a market of servile labor sourced from the Balkans. The concomitance between enslavement and blackness in European countries was both an import from the Muslim world and a belated reality.[37] The myth of Noah's curse of blacks was revived with extreme violence and virulence in the United States in reaction to abolitionist campaigns, notably during the antebellum period and the Civil War. Propaganda in favor of slavery exploded during this time and circulated a veritable gospel of hatred of black men in both the United States and Europe.

After slavery was abolished, racist leagues and associations in countless American states would draw from that massive collection of texts and pamphlets, up until the present day.

The contradiction between universalism and racism has remained unresolved in the modern era. This is evidenced by, for example, the French Republic's difficulty, within its colonial empire, in fully integrating as citizens not only so-called natives, but even the offspring of couples composed of one European and one native inhabitant.[38] The universality of citizenship within the French political space would confront that obstacle repeatedly until the empire was dismantled. Indeed, it took nothing short of the implementation of the Nazi project to trigger an international initiative, following the collapse of the Third Reich and under the auspices of UNESCO, to denounce racial ideologies. Racist thought was condemned for its lack of scientific foundation, proven dangerousness, and incompatibility with principles that recognize the unity of humankind, meaning the universality of human rights.

Genetics as a Challenge for the Humanities and Social Sciences

In academia today, it is easy to see debates about universalism versus heritability of racial characteristics and behaviors as a relic of the past. However, a similar debate is still raging in academic circles in the United States and France. Moral and political censure of racist thought is universal in the academy, but there are still scholars who make claims about heritability that (seem to) contradict today's universalism, or, in other words, make claims that suggest that race is a type of unalterable otherness. Not that long ago, the geneticist James Watson, winner of the 1962 Nobel Prize with Francis Crick and Maurice Wilkins for their description of the DNA double helix, and architect of the international human genome project, sparked an international uproar on the subject. In October 2007, Watson told Britain's *Sunday Times* that biological research had shown that the innate intelligence of blacks was inferior to that of whites. Watson's statements were in fact a continuation of *The Bell Curve*, a 1994 book about performance differences between various "categories" of the American population in tests measuring intellectual quotient, and they reiterated the arguments of an earlier famous article in the *Harvard Educational Review* on the same theme.[39] As I was writing this book, the latest publication by Nicholas Wade was provoking similar, if less widespread, indignation. As it happens, the author is not a researcher, much less a Nobel laureate, but rather a former science columnist for the *New York Times*.[40] This no doubt explains why the outrage sparked by Wade's *A Troublesome Inheritance: Genes, Race, and Human History* only barely reached the other side of the Atlantic. Nonetheless, various magazines, scientific journals, informational websites, and scientific blogs in the United States reported, in vehement and well-argued terms, on Wade's book, which is geared to a general audience and whose theories, in the guise of simplifying advances in genetics and evolutionary psychology, reprise the refrains of ordinary racist thinking. The author's line of reasoning is utterly transparent:

> It is reasonable to assume that if traits like skin color have evolved in a population, the same may be true of its social behavior, and hence the very different kinds of society seen in the various races and in the world's great civilizations differ not just because of their received culture—in other words, in what is learned from birth—but also because of variations in the social behavior of their members, carried down in their genes.[41]

Wade accuses social anthropologists—falsely I might add—
of denying the existence of genetic variations among populations on a global scale. Yet in 1942, Franz Boas's former student
Ashley Montagu, who set out to eliminate use of the term "race"
in both scientific and everyday language after the war, under
UNESCO auspices, and presaging Nicholas Wade's perennial
bête noire today, suggested the following:

> In the genetic sense a race may be defined as a population
> which differs in the incidence of certain genes from other
> populations, with one or more of which it is exchanging or
> is potentially capable of exchanging genes across whatever
> boundaries (usually geographical) may separate them. If
> we are asked whether in this sense there exist a fair num-
> ber of races in the human species, the answer is very defi-
> nitely that there do.[42]

The issue, as will be outlined in the following pages, does not
lie in determining whether variations observed between populations are real or imaginary, but rather in understanding to what
political ends they are used. Even if Wade deplores the horrors
caused by racist thinking, from eugenics to genocide, his aim
is nonetheless to accord collective genetic variations a decisive
role in explaining diversity among societies. An excerpt about
use of the concept of adaptive evolution provides an example of
his methodology (note that the passage has not been cut):

> From a glance at an Eskimo's physique, it is easy to recog-
> nize an evolutionary process at work that has molded the
> human form for better survival in an arctic environment.
> Populations that live at high altitudes, like Tibetans, repre-
> sent another adaptation to extreme environments; in this
> case, the changes in blood cell regulation are less visible but
> have been identified genetically. The adaptation of Jews to

capitalism is another such evolutionary process, though
harder to recognize because the niche to which Jews are
adapted is one that has required a behavioral change, not
a physical one.[43]

Was it necessary to accord such importance to an author
like Nicholas Wade in this book? Judging from the volume of
critical responses to *A Troublesome Inheritance*, from biologists and geneticists for the most part, Wade's book has the
potential to do serious damage to public debate on race. In
France we are inclined to believe that such a book is dangerous. We keep in mind that the reception of the 1975 book *Sociobiology*, written by the entomologist Edward Wilson, has
been very poor indeed. By the end of the 1970s, this new dis-
cipline had been appropriated by and confined to a far-right
think tank, the Research and Study Group for European Civilization (or GRECE, its French acronym). The subsequent
publication of a book by anthropologist Marshall Sahlins that
refuted Wilson's theories, and its unusually quick translation
into French, were equally influential in relegating sociobiology
to a lonely corner of the social sciences.[44] The following year,
1981, a new scientific journal, *Le Genre humain*, came out. Its
first issue was entitled "Science Confronts Racism," and in it
the Nobel biologist François Jacob debunked—he thought
definitively—the scientificity of the notion of race. In the same
issue, a translated posthumous article by Charles Frankel described the landscape of sociobiology in the wake of the publication of *Sociobiology* and *On Human Nature* (1978), also by
Wilson, in measured but radically critical terms.[45]

These challenges to sociobiology in the United States were
no doubt radical in the immediate wake of the publication of
Wilson's book. The debate has yet to abate, as evidenced in
spectacular fashion by Marshall Sahlins's resignation from the

National Academy of Sciences in February 2013 to protest the election of anthropologist Napoleon Chagnon, a proponent of sociobiological theories, as a member.[46] But the discussion in America has not been limited to insults and controversy, for the serious question is that of the porosity of the frontier between the sciences of society and the mind, and the sciences of nature.[47] From France, we can observe that researchers working in the fields of population genetics, evolutionary psychology, animal societies, or human/animal interactions don't claim to belong to a general framework like sociobiology. Conversely, as has become apparent in recent years, the most heated debates have focused on the more or less large degree of culturalism that has been applied to the analysis of social distinctions.[48] In Europe, the distance created between biological determinism and any description of social acts is so powerful that our intellectual debates about racism are reconstructed, perhaps solely, around the question of cultural identity.

{ ⚔ }

Even while most of academia has turned against the notion of race as a heritable social or behavioral characteristic, sociobiology is far from dying out, especially in the United States. In redefining race, as this book aims to do, sociobiology is a school of thought with which one must contend. The academic sphere is not alone in linking genetic descriptors to the formation of social identities—far from it. Biosociological inferences serve as arguments for commercial labs that target individuals seeking reassurance of what they believe to be their true origins. In France and the United States, the iGENEA company, for example, offers to answer the question "Are you Jewish?" (the same for Irish, Basque, and other origins) by using a DNA test, or rather three tests of varying quality (basic, premium,

expert) and increasing cost. The rationale used in their advertising is worth attention:

> Based on your specific genetic characteristics, we can iden-
> tify whether you are of Jewish descent, which line the Jew-
> ish descent is from (paternal, maternal or both lines) and
> even to what percentage you are Jewish. In addition, your
> profile is compared with more than 700,000 people in our
> database. If we find a genetic match, i.e., people with whom
> you correspond genetically, you may contact these people
> and intensify your family research.[49]

The subtext here is that users of this service can meet partners
with similar genetic heritage through this site. Though meant
to allow users to find family to whom they are already related,
this service also allows users who are interested in marrying
within their own groups to find partners. To begin, the notion
of engineering premarital encounters through a database of
"genetic matches" is laughable: iGENEA seems also to want to
be an overspecialized dating website. Nonetheless, the company bolsters its list of services with a bibliography composed
of a mix of studies and articles with no scientific basis and
serious texts on the identification of genetic markers with a
significant presence among certain Jewish populations. (The
bibliography is composed exclusively of American sources.)
Similarly, the Genetic Literacy Project (GLP), which claims
to provide scientific information on human genetic markers,
as well as on the innocuousness of GMO use in farming and
on food hygiene, creates a thick fog within which scientific
data can be muddled with columns and ordinary opinion.[50]
According to its mission statement, "The GLP explores the
intersection of DNA research and real world applications of
genetics with media and policy to disentangle science from
ideology," meaning it can post articles drawn from an odd mix

of publications, with no apparent hierarchy, in the name of scientific endeavor. GLP spokesman Jon Entine, a journalist and publicist, gained notoriety by publishing works on the racial dimension of Jewish identity and the innately exceptional performance of black athletes.[51] Under the guise of axiological antiracism, Entine's books career between various approximations drawn from multiple scientific journals, used to defend the thesis of the profound or essential character of genetic differences in determining behavior and exceptional traits in certain communities and groups, as opposed to the superficial effects of social or cultural distinctions.[52]

Companies that offer to retrace their clients' lineages on the basis of a DNA sample adjust their biological analyses according to data gathered from the client's own memory and historical knowledge of the past spatial mobility of their ancestors. Nothing could be more legitimate, particularly when dealing with a lineage that left no written trace. But while one may be sympathetic to this type of search, it remains difficult to justify the obfuscated lines of reasoning that lead to its conclusions about geographical origins: where are the feelings of the subjects, the intuitions, the genetic markers, the certitudes? In this case, neither the study of genetic heritage nor historical research arouses suspicion; the fact that both are invoked in scientific arguments whose systems of cause and effect are incomprehensible does.[53] This indicates that despite progress in the field of genetic analysis, research on specific profiles still produces little but "blurred vision(s)" and "imprecise separations," to cite Albert Jacquard.[54] In the United States, criticism of these biotechnological practices has focused on the risk of encouraging "ethnic absolutism and primordialism."[55] The debate is ongoing.

Moving beyond the concerns raised by companies offering genetic reconstitutions of family histories, we can also observe a worrisome shift in the legitimate arena of universities, laboratories, and scientific journals. The receptiveness to the article "Natural History of Ashkenazi Intelligence" (or at least its dissemination) demonstrates that sociobiological arguments continue to find a place within scientific discussions, in this instance a journal distributed by Cambridge University Press.[56] The article postulates the existence of significant correlations between data compiled from medical literature on the presence of certain diseases (like Tay-Sachs disease) in highly endogamous Ashkenazi societies, and analyses related to the sociocultural history of European Judaism in the Middle Ages; these correlations are as vague as they are arbitrary, not to mention at times ludicrous. The authors draw the following conclusion:

> High IQ test scores of Ashkenazim, along with their unusual pattern of abilities, are a product of natural selection, stemming from their occupation of an unusual social niche. All the required preconditions—low inward gene flow and unusually high reproductive reward for certain cognitive skills, over a long-enough period—did exist. These preconditions are both necessary and sufficient, so such a selective process would almost inevitably have this kind of result.[57]

Though they acknowledge that demographic data about European Jews during the early Middle Ages is scarce, the article's authors nonetheless propose a battery of inferences: All the Jews of this era, or at least the large majority of them, had occupations that demanded an IQ equal or superior to 100. And among Jews, as in the rest of the population, rich families had greater reproductive rates than poor ones. Finally, wealthy Jewish families led by someone with a cognitively demanding

profession were particularly fertile. The article even establishes a link between IQ and reproductive capacity:

> Another plausible scenario is that individuals with IQ lower
> than 80, i.e. individuals who could not join the United
> States army because of low IQ, could not find spouses: it
> is likely that such individuals could not participate in the
> early medieval Ashkenazi economy and simply drifted
> away from their natal ethnicity to become farmers or to find
> other work.[58]

With a hypothesis like the incapacity of people with low
IQs to marry, it is indeed possible to construct any number
of scenarios, especially when you throw in various series of
statistical indicators. The hypotheses expressed in the article "Natural History of Ashkenazi Intelligence" are similar to
those in another article on the same subject, which appeared
in *Commentary*. Author Charles Murray ponders the question
of what became of Jews of low intelligence over the course of
history in order to better understand how selection occurred
in favor of Jews of very high intelligence in the context of a
hypothetical decline of the Jewish population in late antiquity.
Starting with the transformation of Judaism to a religion of
the book, following the destruction of the Second Temple and the
end of ceremonial rites and public sacrifices, Murray offers the
following explanation:

> It is not necessary to maintain that Jews of low intelli-
> gence were run out of town because they could not read
> the Torah and commentaries fluently. Rather, few people
> enjoy being in a position where their inadequacies are con-
> stantly highlighted. It is human nature to withdraw from
> such situations. I suggest that the Jews who fell away from
> Judaism from the 1st to 6th centuries C.E. were heavily

concentrated among those who could not learn to read well enough to be good Jews—meaning those from the lower half of the intelligence distribution. Even before the selection pressures arising from urban occupations began to have an effect, I am arguing, the remaining self-identified Jews circa 800 C.E. already had elevated intelligence.[59]

How can we take the medicogenetic and statistical portions of this argument seriously, even based as they are on the study of samples taken from people suffering from the same genetic diseases, when the sociohistorical correlations appear so far-fetched? Is using IQ levels in a positive way (in favor of Jews) better than using them negatively (against blacks)? Starting from the idea that Jews found themselves confined to a "niche"—as Nicholas Wade does, as discussed above—the three authors of "Natural History of Ashkenazi Intelligence" believe they are providing evidence of the genetic transmission of intellectual faculties considered to be adapted to the social functions performed by Jews in European societies since the Middle Ages. Not only was this study published in a scientific journal, but publications like the *New York Times* and the *Economist* gave it coverage rarely granted an article from an academic journal.[60] This should be taken as an indication that in the United States and Great Britain sociobiological arguments are viewed as legitimate by leading media outlets with high intellectual standards. In this case, it becomes clear that the passage cited earlier on the respective niches occupied by Eskimos, Tibetans, and Jews expresses nothing that is particularly anti-Semitic. One wonders which is worse.

"How Jews Became Smart: Anti-'Natural History of Ashkenazi Intelligence,'"[61] by anthropologist R. Brian Ferguson, offers a comprehensive critique of the entire argumentation behind "Natural History of Ashkenazi Intelligence." Ferguson's arguments prove far more solid and well reasoned than those he addresses. Rather than challenging the article's institutional legitimacy and success with derision, Ferguson focuses on demonstrating its scientific fallacies via counterarguments related to the spectrum of disciplines on which the authors draw: population and evolutionary genetics, neurobiology, the psychology of intellectual quotients, and the history of medieval Judaism. Without summarizing all the elements of Ferguson's thorough rebuttal, let's examine the specific role of history in his deconstruction of the sociobiological approach. The Ashkenazi reproductive model imagined by the authors of "Natural History of Ashkenazi Intelligence" relies on the notion that the rich-and-intelligent reproduced more than the dumb-and-poor, and that the sociopsychological profile of the former group enabled it to dominate the latter from a demographical perspective, and that every generation in the era in question saw average IQs in the community rise (and be passed down through the genes of lucky candidates). However, the authors did not take into account sociohistorical scholarship on medieval Jewish communities that reveals the existence of deep internal stratification, as well as revealing that the ideal type of a rich, highly educated, and shrewdly political banker was appropriate to only a small elite within these societies. Ferguson writes:

> In sum, for centuries, a wealthy, self-consciously aristocratic, intermarrying elite conducted the lion's share of business, controlled financial courts, determined tax rates, acted as intermediaries with political authorities, determined who could live where, administered economic matters and community property, and filled secular and rabbinical offices.[62]

That there was only a small elite who fits the description the article attempted to apply to all Jews shows that the idea that Jews as a group, self-selected for intelligence, does not stand up to scrutiny. Ferguson's conclusion on the scientific and public success of the article "Natural History of Ashkenazi Intelligence" serves as a warning:

> [The article] and its public reaction should be of concern to anthropologists. They challenge more than a century of anthropology premised on psychic unity, the idea that humans are all born with essentially similar mental capabilities. They illustrate just how marginal cultural anthropology has become in wider public discourse. For a long time, it has been common to hear, in everyday conversations, that genes explain behavior—of individuals, of humans in general, of women, of men, or of races, although the last may only be whispered. But we have not commonly heard that same idea applied to ethnic or national differences. We are right on the edge of that now. This is the whole point of [Nicholas] Wade's *New York Times* article [March 12, 2006]. Where *The New York Times* leads, others follow. We have a very short distance to go before it becomes "common knowledge" that "scientists have shown that different peoples are just born different in how they act."[63]

The scientific literature Ferguson refers to in order to construct his counterargument is vast for a number of reasons—also historical—that are addressed in Harry Ostrer's work on the history of genetic research on Jewish populations.[64] To begin with, Jewish populations were the subject of numerous genetic studies long before DNA was understood, because of the frequency of endogamy attributed to them, as well as to the Sardinians, which allowed for a number of hypotheses to be tested. Then, postulation of a specific historical and ethnic unity among Jewish populations became a major political issue in the contemporary era in diametrically opposed ways: raciological anti-Semitism on the one hand and the Zionist project on the other. Finally, beginning in the 1920s, a large number of preeminent genetic researchers in both the United States and Israel came from Jewish families. The vast amount of scientific literature produced at the convergence of these circumstances does not justify—and therein lies the interest and merit of Ferguson's work—the inferences evoked in "Natural History of Ashkenazi Intelligence" concerning the hypothesis of a specific Jewish IQ.

Ferguson comes to the defense of social and cultural anthropology with brio, as Marshall Sahlins once did, despite the climate of scientific intimidation surrounding the field of sociobiology. As a historian, I want to note that my field does not include study of the IQs of individuals. However, historical analysis can incorporate the processes that drive individuals and populations to act in one way or another. In a recent work, Noah Efron asks a question that, from a historical point of view, is the exact opposite of an approach based on the genetics of intelligence: Why are so many high-level twentieth-century scientists Jewish?[65] First, the phenomenon Efron attempts to explain can be described objectively: number of chairs and laboratory directorships, patents and inventions, Nobel Prizes, and so on. Next, his approach reflects that of a historian situating the phenomena in question in specific periods and settings. Like Ferguson, Efron challenges the article "Natural History of Ashkenazi Intelligence" and its foundation of unsubstantiated inferences. Until more information is available, the role of genetics in explaining intellectual performance remains in the spectrum of ideological hypothesis. But Efron also rejects the somewhat vague culturalist approach that explains the scientific performance of numerous Jewish scientists in the twentieth century as the consequence of seventeen centuries of the valorization of Talmudic expertise within Jewish societies. Sticking with the here and now, Efron emphasizes that Jewish participation in the development of major scientific disciplines was minimal until the last quarter of the nineteenth century in both Europe and the United States. His aim is therefore to understand what caused such a "disproportionate" Jewish presence in scientific milieus using three case studies: the early twentieth-century United States, the Soviet Union beginning in the 1920s, and the State of Israel beginning with its establishment. Efron's analysis integrates sociopolitical and sociocultural parameters specific to each society. Historical factors, a few of which are noted here, enter into the historical explanation of the phenomenon in question: the anti-Semitic *numerus clausus* of American universities, the fact that many Jews born in the Russian Empire were both well-read and opposed to the tsarist regime, and the momentum of political Zionism. This method completely rejects all forms of sociobiology as well as even the most essentialist versions of the cultural approach. The way Efron constructs his problematic and conducts his investigation convincingly illustrates what historians can contribute to any social science study on the specific traits of communities or populations. Efron's book is a case study of why historical inquiry is an essential tool for building an understanding of race. As we have seen from "Natural History of Ashkenazi Intelligence," it is easy to espouse ideas about race that are supposedly based on historical evidence but that in fact either are outright false or fail to take into account specific political and cultural circumstances. They come to unsubstantiated conclusions. For these reasons historical research is important to achieving a true understanding of race. It is only though careful historical research that we can contextualize claims about culture and group characteristics, and avoid false and ultimately harmful mythologies, such as the idea that medieval Jews self-selected for intelligence, and supposedly scientific claims about inherited, inescapable difference.

Thirty years after the publication of Franz Boas's *Race, Language and Culture*, hematologist Jacques Ruffié established the "physical anthropology" chair at the Collège de France, which he held from 1972 to 1992. In his inaugural lecture, this tireless and fierce opponent of sociobiology[66] reversed the burden of causality from the social sciences to medical knowledge, rather than the inverse—all the while affirming the efficacy of blood markers to identify, for example, ancient migration:

> Physical anthropology now has the methods to analyze, with great precision, the structure and evolution of human groups. It shows us the importance of culture in the biological fate of populations and the fragility of the equilibrium that allowed humanity to reach as far as it has. But the very precision of physical anthropology reveals its limits. It describes but doesn't explain; it addresses phenomena whose origins it cannot identify. It will fall to social anthropology, ethnology, and prehistory to reveal their causes. Together, these fields will form the "science of man," still in its infancy, but which now appears to be indispensable.[67]

This assertion occupies a prominent spot in Ruffié's demonstration, as evidenced by its placement in the second-to-last paragraph of the text. His inversion of causalities in scientific reasoning allows us to combine understanding of human societies with understanding of human physiologies without leaving ourselves vulnerable to the slightest sociobiological derivative, thus curtailing any possible raciological inference.

Ruffié's position appears all the more indispensable given that modern-day knowledge has eliminated two approximate arguments previously employed by the social sciences to refute sociobiological reasoning. First, it has been established that the old polygenic hypothesis unknowingly corresponded to the historical reality of the contemporaneity and interaction between two distinct human species: Neanderthal and modern man.[68] Of course, that discovery in no way modifies the moral reprobation merited by polygenic theorizing that, in the course of its intellectual and political development, invented natural distinctions among modern men. Second, the natural sciences historically dismissed the possibility of the heritability of acquired characteristics by relying on a past stage of experimental biology that denied all retroaction from the history of a body to the genetic material it carried. Yet that scientific trend directly conflicts with advances in contemporary genetic biology, notably pertaining to the genetic transmission of trauma that occurs in the first moments of a subject's existence.[69] What lessons can be drawn from these two transformations in social scientific reasoning? Paleoanthropology and genetic biology no longer provide the scientific arguments—or even, one could argue, the scientists—that would provide ultimate proof of the absurdity of racist hypotheses. But the elimination of this overarching insurance policy is good news for social and human sciences, namely because as a direct result, these fields are pushed to construct scientific arguments—and their political extensions—against racial thought based uniquely on social research on human societies.

The Constructivist Model and Its Mottos

Regardless of the perturbations introduced by sociobiological ideology in the countries and milieus that have granted it a place, the humanities and social sciences rely, without notable exception, on a foundation that for lack of a better alternative we can qualify as constructivism in principle. This approach has engaged much of academic research and has been widely addressed in public debate. Constructivism, in this context, is the view that aspects of human definition like race and gender are not inborn, biologically determined features but rather social fictions that are constructed within a given society. In their valuable study of the question of race in contemporary philosophy and social science, Magali Bessone and Daniel Sabbagh provide a substantial analysis of the scientific impact of the constructivist stance.[70] Without reproducing their entire argument here, it's worth noting that the constructivist perspective finds its rhetorical translation in the success of the formula "we are not born x, we become it" in all manner of texts and mediums. For example, two recent works boast titles that borrow the formula: *We Are Not Born Black, We Become It*.[71] The first addresses the long history of the construction of racial prejudice against black individuals, while the second deals with the condition imposed on people of African origin in French society and the manner in which those concerned define their situation themselves. The formula cited above had already been used, in reference to black citizens in Canada, by the novelist Dany Laferrière in his first book.[72] It is a very effective communication tool, as attested to by the following text presenting the soccer player Lilian Thuram's Education against Racism Foundation on its website and in leaflets:

> We are not born racist, we become one. This truth is the cornerstone of the Foundation: Education against Racism. Racism is above all an intellectual construction. We must realize that history has conditioned us from generation to generation, to see ourselves primarily as blacks, whites, North Africans, Asians.[73]

The same phrase reworked in the completely opposite sense was recently brandished by Italy's racist far right. On May 21, 2013, Cécile Kyenge, Italian Congo-born minister for integration, refused to shake hands with a member of the Northern League after its elected representatives had viciously verbally attacked her. As a consequence, she was the subject of a vengeful statement from the extremist, racist movement Forza Nuova. The neo-fascist organization inverted the formula in its statement:

> Forza Nuova expresses its solidarity with the leader of the Northern League group, reiterates its opposition to any form of multiethnic society and recognition of *ius soli*. One is born Italian, one doesn't become it.[74]

In French political and intellectual collective memory, and indeed well beyond our borders, the adage "we aren't born x, we become it" evokes a famous passage from Simone de Beauvoir's *The Second Sex*:

> One is not born, but rather becomes, woman. No biological, psychic, or economic destiny defines the figure that the human female takes on in society; it is civilization as a whole that elaborates this intermediary product between the male and the eunuch that is called feminine.[75]

The shift from a topic at that time designated as "sex," and today more commonly as gender, toward that of race was all the more natural and legitimate given that Beauvoir's text itself suggests a homology between sexism and racism:

> To prove women's inferiority, antifeminists began to draw not only, as before, on religion, philosophy, and theology but also on science: biology, experimental psychology, and so forth. At most they were willing to grant "separate but

equal status" to the *other* sex. That winning formula is most significant: it is exactly that formula the Jim Crow Laws put into practice with regard to black Americans; this so-called egalitarian segregation served only to introduce the most extreme forms of discrimination. This convergence is in no way pure chance: whether it is race, caste, class, or sex reduced to an inferior condition, the justification process is the same. "The eternal feminine" corresponds to "the black soul" or "the Jewish character."[76]

Historical research has not always neglected the importance of such analogies. For example, in the 1960s and 1970s, Charles Ralph Boxer, a renowned specialist of the Portuguese and Dutch Empires, successively examined the phenomena of racialization and manifestations of misogyny in the colonial era.[77] More recently, the links established between those two categories, as well as several others, have inspired a number of research projects that confirm their rigor and relevance.[78] The philosophical and ideological rejection of "differentialism" presents itself as universalism in principle. But that universal perspective collides with history—an ensemble of social processes that produce differences and establish them as facts of nature (or simply declare that indelible markers exist). Within the context of the homologous relationship that can be established between sexism and racism, Beauvoir's feminism can be considered in relationship to the antiracism or anticolonialism expressed by an author like Frantz Fanon.[79] It's therefore not surprising that the interpretation of Frantz Fanon's works as a call for the removal of distinctions within the human condition, and as a result as universalism, would include comparisons to Simone de Beauvoir's propositions, even going so far as to borrow her famous formula, as some scholars have done in considering Fanon's work:

Though Fanon had almost essentialized the difference between the body experiences of the Black and the White, this difference was grounded in a social and historical context and was the result of a lived experience, not an ontological flaw: one is not born Black but becomes Black, to paraphrase de Beauvoir.[80]

De Beauvoir recycled a trope of religious and philosophical reasoning, present in Western writing since the Church Fathers, to define her constructivist position. The expression can be found in texts by Tertullian (*Fiunt, non nascuntur Christiani,* "Christians are made, not born"),[81] Erasmus (*Homines, mihi crede, non nascuntur, sed finguntur,* "Believe me, men are not born, they are made"),[82] and Spinoza (*Homines enim civiles non nascuntur, sed fiunt,* "Men are not born fit for citizenship, but must be made so").[83] In the case of social construction of blackness, the expression can be applied to a range of different phenomena. Some are very simple, for example when African migrants who have never self-identified as "black" in their countries of origin discover, once in North America or Europe, that it is the first descriptor assigned them. A Sudanese professor, in order to understand the processes through which he became black upon moving to Canada, proposed undertaking an "ethnography [of] the processes of becoming black. That is, the cultural, linguistic, and socio-psychic implications of what it means to possess the Black body in North America (and the Western world in general)."[84]

Awad Ibrahim's research into his own experience prompted him to define race according to a constructivist frame of reference:

> Race, I contend, is a network of meanings against which we negotiate our psychic being . . . or a collection of stories we "tell" ourselves and others.[85]

Anthropologist Verena Stolcke entitled one of her best-known articles "Los mestizos no nacen, se hacen," which can be safely translated as: "One is not born mestizo, one becomes it."[86]

We can also consider the production of ethnic identities prompted by the need to give substance to existing definitions of categories of populations as defined by law.[87] In certain contexts, negotiation over ethnic belonging constitutes the very fabric of social life, as revealed by historians and anthropologists. For example, a study conducted on the implementation of article 68 of the Brazilian Constitution of 1988, which concerns the attribution of land to communities whose residents are reportedly the descendants of fugitive African slaves (*quilombolas*), revealed that local groups defined themselves using the requirements established by administrative officials and a committee of experts. Their self-definition is built on ethnic and genealogical identity that is not only emotional or psychic, but also dependent, when required, on changeable public policy. In this case, one is not born *quilombola*, one becomes it.[88] This kind of approach is not limited to the fabrication of blackness. To the contrary, historians and sociologists over the past thirty years have taken an interest in the processes by which populations become "white." This research is not about the phenotypic impact of the arrival of European migrants in an America where native and African populations were the majority. Rather, it is primarily concerned with the attribution of the "white" descriptor to descendants of Europeans from the colonial era and later to dominated migrant populations during the contemporary era (Irish, Italians, Jews).[89] But the solidification of the "whiteness" of people living in the American colonies also reflects a form of reassurance for those facing the risk of transformation at the frontiers of overseas European societies. Novels of captivity and life on the frontier showcase the processes by which their protagonists discover their whiteness at the exact moment when their identity in the "wilderness" is faltering.[90] The same formula may have been used to incorporate more or less fluid modes of identification of mixed-race populations, for example in Spanish America.

Any analysis of practices of assignation and the self-definition of human beings in terms of natural identity also concerns phenomena less visible than the movement for reparations for slavery and less dramatic than the shock of international migration. For Brazilian psychoanalyst Neusa Santos Souza, regardless of an individual's generation of belonging, his or her self-identification as black stems from an effort to update a constructed, never entirely innate, concept of blackness:

> Being black means becoming aware of an ideological process that, starting from a mythical discourse about the self, produces a structure of unfamiliarity that imprisons the individual within an alienated image he or she recognizes as their own. Being black means taking possession of this awareness and creating a new awareness, which reinforces the respect for differences and reaffirms the dignity of the other beyond the level of exploitation. Thus, being black is not an inherent, *a priori* condition. It's a state of becoming. Being black means becoming black.[91]

Whether we adopt a philosophical perspective or merely employ common sense, it's not difficult to see that perception of alterity results from a process of self-identification as much as from an attribution imposed by others.

As the reader will see in the following pages, it is perhaps precisely the persistent phenomenon of "sameness in the other" that fuels racial policies. After all, the way we regard domesticated or wild animals is quite often far more generous than the way reserved for human populations scarcely different than our own. A shared humanity can also act as an aggravating factor. In her study on racism, Lydia Flem cites a famous article by Sigmund Freud that analyses "uncanny strangeness," meaning the strangeness that manifests itself in the midst of the most familiar experiences.[92] The text recounts an anecdote according to which Freud, during a train voyage, believed that an intruder had entered his compartment when it was in fact his own reflection in the mirror. Lydia Flem creates a parallel between this story and a remark by psychoanalyst Jean-Bertrand Pontalis:

> So, when does one experience dread before the foreigner? When the other is at the same time similar and different. That is why I maintain that the accepted idea that racism reflects a radical rejection of the other, a fundamental intolerance of differences, etc., is false, or in any case incomplete. Contrary to what we believe, the image of the same, the double, is infinitely more troubling than that of the other.[93]

Thus, the constructivist point of view is not only the best way to deny all credit to social theories that are based on genetic pseudodeterminations to describe and distinguish the diversity of men. It is also a framework of analysis that invites us to describe every social phenomenon in terms of process, that is, of historical transformation. On the one hand, it denies any essentialist conception of identities, and, on the other hand, it invites us to not excessively oppose identity and otherness. In this also it is very valuable to produce research on racial categorization.

Political Consistencies

Imagine a web of connections between historiographical approaches and political positions on race as a political resource, in such a way that they all appear coherent. Interestingly three coherent models or ideal types emerge.

First, the model with the greatest chronological depth, which stretches from Hippocratic musings on climates and the nature-based Aristotelian justification of slavery to the politicization of discoveries in genetics, and from the Greeks to conquering Christendom to the contemporary era: This range coincides with the broad question of how alterity was handled. Given the diversity of political, social, religious, and economic configurations tackled within this framework, the political corollary of this academic approach should be an extremely open conception of racial domination. However, this broad definition incurs the risk of being unable to distinguish between instances of domination that entail the attribution of natural inferiority (or harmfulness) and those that simply reflect a process of socioeconomic, sociopolitical, or socioreligious differentiation. If every instance of collective discrimination entails racial logic, how can we not substantiate the existence of forms of racism that are anti-young, anti-old, anti-proletariat, and so on? In other words, intellectual coherence dictates that once we broaden the pertinent chronological scope to the entirety of historical periods, roughly speaking, we will find ourselves in the position of considering that a greater number of types of collective hostility and social discrimination are racist.

Second, a model that stretches over the shortest duration and whose scope is confined to the formalization of contemporary racial theories drawn from modern biological theories on heredity: In this case, historical study is dictated by identification of constructed arguments within sweeping racialist narratives, which imitate or mime those found in the experimental sciences. At the same time, this model entails chasing a (nearly) inaccessible object: a racism that is, dare we say, chemically pure, or at the least a system of domination in which racial criteria overwhelm all other markers. Nazism would be the sole system to come close to matching this description. The corollary of this historiographical approach is therefore a position that attempts to limit the political scope of racism to theories clearly rooted in the lexicology of biology and genetics. That restriction risks giving rise to a form of color blindness or recognizing racism beyond skin color, insofar that a policy need only reflect a clear and comprehensible biologizing foundation in order to be regarded as racist. Yet, we know that contemporary racism is even more effective beyond the biologizing frame when racial vocabulary is excluded from the political arena, at least in countries like modern-day France and Germany. In order to remain coherent, historians who limit the field of racial categories to public expression of concepts based on experimental biology cannot classify contemporary manifestations of collective discrimination today as racist, since they all lack or avoid references to the natural sciences.

And, finally, the approach proposed here: On the basis of persecutory practices against minority groups regulated in the Western Christian world since the thirteenth century, the phenomenon of collective conversions kindled the desire within the Iberian Peninsula to differentiate minorities that had become undetectable. The need to reveal a difference that had become imperceptible led to the creation of descriptions of targeted identities in terms of lineage, genealogy, and finally, nature. This political matrix can be active or dormant, but it has been reactivated on multiple occasions since the fifteenth century. Paradoxically, this model was also applied, at least in part, to the management of relations between European settlers and Native American populations, Africans deported to the New World, and closely administered Asian communities. It has since become an active element of expressions of hostility to postcolonial migrants. This historiographical argument should correlate to a concept of racism within politics that does not translate all forms of domination or segregation in terms of race. Within that framework, amalgamations between nature and culture, both explicit and implicit, must be considered with a particularly watchful and critical eye. Or more precisely, the focus should remain on the naturalization of sociopolitical differences, be they real or imaginary. This process of naturalization can, at the minimum, be limited to the use of naturalist metaphors in political language. But its effectiveness can prove to be gravely harmful. The harm of these systems of assumptions and inferences based on naturalistic ideologies is measured in terms of hierarchical distrust, all forms of segregation, paralysis of the critical analysis of social or political phenomenon, and the distortion of observations of socioeconomic tensions. Finally, to sum up the model of historiographical interpretation proposed in this book, the historian must refuse to reduce everything to racial oppression, while remaining cognizant of the validity and efficacy of racial questions in social and political life.

CHAPTER TWO

Historiographical Debate

Toward a Larger History of Race and Racism

As indicated by its title, this book is focused on the role that historical research can, or rather should, play in the elucidation of political processes through which populations and individuals found and find themselves categorized in relation to race, and subsequently discriminated against, subjugated, persecuted, and even exterminated. By examining these processes, historians can shed light on how and when societies, in specific times and places, have created and perpetuated racial distinctions and implemented racist policies. Therefore, it is in no way meant to evaluate the coherence of arguments and demonstrations at the margins of the biological and social sciences. That said, as soon as political history touches on a subject like the formation of racial categories, it must evaluate to what extent its agenda can be determined in relation to that of the history of the sciences. Notwithstanding a rather general agreement between historians, which consists of excluding any sociobiology-inspired proposals, nothing could be less cohesive than historical analyses of the apparition of political ideologies and social practices that produce distinctions according to race. Even defining the object of study is subject to broad variations. In space: Is isolating the Western case relevant when racial prejudices and caste rigidity are present in many other regions and cultures? In time: Should the investigation be limited to the period during which social theories were experiencing the intellectual pull of the natural sciences, followed by that of experimental biology?

From the French perspective, the domain of social sciences that analyzes racial categorization and discrimination appears to be crushed beneath the weight of a vast library of articles, studies, and, of course, digital materials produced by Anglophone academic institutions. This accumulation of available information seems intimidating at first glance, in two notable ways. First, the ease with which the English term "race" is established as the object of study contrasts with the French inhibition in using this word. Second, when we consider the sheer volume of scholarship available and the mobilization of a vast spectrum of disciplines, including philosophy, demography, political science, ethnology, comparative literature, and sociology, it's clear that a groundswell of research on questions of race within the social and human sciences has taken place in the United States and other Anglophone countries. There is no equivalent, in pedagogical, scientific, or editorial terms, in France, at least for now.

However, exploration of this Anglophone body of work does render it less intimidating, namely because despite the enormity of what has been produced, certain internal limitations are quickly apparent. For example, research on other periods and societies occupies a relatively marginal spot when compared to the number of studies that focus exclusively on the contemporary history of the United States and the imperial and postcolonial history of Great Britain. In this regard, reading the latest edition of the *Encyclopædia Britannica* can be enlightening—as it only considers race for the following three cases: the American South after the Civil War, apartheid in South Africa, and postcolonial conflicts on British soil. As a result, Anglophone universities rarely draw on research conducted in other academic environments. Even if the American racial experience rightly constitutes a major object of study for the humanities and social sciences, it can in no way be generalized. The rigor of a situational approach to social and cultural phenomena demands that the case of the United States be taken for what it is: one case. In addition, the inward-looking nature of Anglophone intellectual production has prompted the majority of researchers to base their studies on a nearly perfect equivalence between race and color, in reference to the African American condition in a post-slavery society. Yet that equivalence is not self-evident, a point that will be discussed at length in the following pages.

The undeniable importance of black/white race issues in social and political life in the United States does not mean the scope of social science research should be restricted to a black/white opposition, even in the US context, and scholars are already expanding research beyond this dichotomy. Specialists who study other minority populations and more recent migrations are demanding that the spectrum of research be enlarged. Here is a plea, chosen from among many, for a greater expansion of the field of race scholarship by legal expert Juan F. Perea:

> The most pervasive and powerful paradigm of race in the United States is the black/white binary paradigm. I define this paradigm as the conception that race in America consists, either exclusively or primarily, of only two constituent racial groups, the black and the white. Many scholars of race reproduce this paradigm when they write and act as though *only the black and the white races matter* for purposes of discussing race and social policy with regard to race. The

mere recognition that "other people of color" exist, without careful attention to their voices, their histories, and their real presence, is merely a reassertion of the black/white paradigm. If one conceives of race and racism as primarily of concern only to blacks and whites, and understands "other people of color" only through some unclear analogy to the "real" races, this just restates the binary paradigm with a slight concession to demographics. . . . The "normal science" of race scholarship specifies inquiry into the relationship between blacks and whites as the exclusive aspect of race relations that needs to be explored and elaborated.[1]

A useful, not to mention symptomatic, example can be found in the "Race" entry in the *Stanford Encyclopedia of Philosophy* (winter 2012 online edition). Unsurprisingly, the bibliography does not include a single title from the humanities or social sciences outside Anglophone academia, not even in translation. In addition, following an introduction on the history of racial categories from Aristotle's time to the Enlightenment, the majority of cases to which the article's theoretical and sociological approach refers are from the United States and are primarily focused on the African American experience, with a few notes on Latinos and Jews. This perspective is entirely legitimate and meets all the criteria for coherence—provided it is presented as localized in and focused on a particular region.

However, the article's opening lines don't appear to recognize these limitations. Instead, they outline a clearly articulated and comprehensible definition of the notion of race in general:

The concept of race has historically signified the division of humanity into a small number of groups based upon five criteria: (1) Races reflect some type of biological foundation, be it Aristotelian essences or modern genes; (2) This biological foundation generates discrete racial groupings, such that all and only all members of one race share a set of biological characteristics that are not shared by members of other races; (3) This biological foundation is inherited from generation to generation, allowing observers to identify an individual's race through her ancestry or genealogy; (4) Genealogical investigation should identify each race's geographic origin, typically in Africa, Europe, Asia, or North and South America; and (5) This inherited racial biological foundation manifests itself primarily in physical phenotypes, such as skin color, eye shape, hair texture, and bone structure, and perhaps also behavioral phenotypes, such as intelligence or delinquency.[2]

The fourth and fifth criteria of this definition require commentary. The proposed geographical division corresponds to a listing of four of the five continents according to the most traditional notions of geography, which may attract scholarly interest as an object of historical study but not as an analytical framework.[3] Furthermore, this continental decoupage doesn't match the distribution of human types imagined by the authors of pictures of human races. None of the major racial classifications, beginning with François Bernier's 1684 contribution, respect this division by continent; they certainly don't reflect current theories on the differentiation of migrant human societies from a shared African origin. According to the fifth criterion of this conceptual definition of "race," the primary manifestation of racial difference relies on the existence of differentiated physical phenotypes. That assertion is the predictable result of a theoretical line of reasoning that draws primarily from a succession of empirical questions focused on the African American experience. The article emphasizes the translation of intrinsic differences into phenotype. It mobilizes the notion of physical phenotype, meaning singular bodily characteristics that can be perceived immediately by the senses. By doing so, the definition dismisses the hypothesis that racial thought can compensate for the paucity of signs of difference in physical phenotype. This point is without a doubt the most disputable, and it will come up repeatedly throughout this book. But the article also evokes the notion of "behavioral phenotypes," which, in medical and biological literature, designate a group of symptoms of mental impairment of genetic origin. The *Stanford Encyclopedia of Philosophy* suggests, quite rightly, that the concept of behavioral phenotypes deployed in racial thinking completely surpassed and perverted the scope of its medical usage in order to designate behavior or social attitudes that had nothing to do with the syndromes thus designated. The question of a "behavioral phenotype" for intelligence corresponds to scholarship on the genetic basis of the intellectual performance of the dominant group in the United States (white Anglo-Saxon Protestants), as well as that of Jews, as previously noted, whereas—indeed, it's hard to miss—the behavioral phenotype for delinquency evokes crime rates observed among the African American population.

With this book, I am gambling on the conviction that historians can contribute to the discussion of phenomena that all too often appear to be viewed in a narrowly contemporary or immediate context. A longer history of race is necessary, and such historical studies will show that race is not necessarily linked to physical phenotypes. In a recent essay, philosopher Claude-Olivier Doron and historian Jean-Paul Lallemand-Stempak discussed four works published in 2012–13 on the impact of contemporary genomics on the social sciences and public policy in the United States. It's worth citing the beginning of their conclusion:

> We can conclude our review of these otherwise remarkable studies with one regret: There is a notable absence among

the abundance of disciplines invited to contribute to these works, which is all the more striking given its omnipresence, meaning that it is frequently referred to in order to characterize what are regarded as "advances" and "ruptures" between the "traditional concept of race" and current events. This absence is *history*. Not one historian was solicited to clarify and expand the at times simplistic vision of the history of the concept of race that serves as the backdrop to this research.[4]

The fact that no historian was included in studies dedicated to the scientific intersections between genetics and the social sciences attests above all to the segmentation that too often separates the social sciences and the humanities in many American universities. As a historian attentive to proposals from the social sciences as a whole, I would like to flesh out a line of reasoning that sheds light on the formation of racial categories in the West, in the capacity of political resources used from the late Middle Ages to the current day. As will be seen, the question of chronological markers occupies a central place in the arguments that I am submitting for debate. That said, the reader will not find a linear path that follows the evolution of the formation of racial categories between the chronological markers indicated above. This is not a synopsis of the history of racism, but rather an invitation to develop the subject of the formation of racial categories as a historical problematic worth examining and that demands significant chronological depth.

Race: Object or Category?

In order to conduct a controlled historiographical study of the formation of racial categories, it is indispensable to first agree on certain definitions. I began to define race and racism at the beginning of the previous chapter, when laying out my agenda for this book, but these definitions deserve a closer look in the context of existing scholarship on the subject. In the social sciences, the theoretical quest for definitions most often creates an obstacle to critical reflection. However, in this instance, clarification is made necessary by the considerable gap in usage and the meaning of the term "race" between the Anglophone and Francophone social sciences. Several brief clarifications may help dissipate the imprecision created by the distance between these two contexts. That said, historical semantics should not be used as an authoritative justification when assigning definitions to concepts.[5] The point is not to date the appearance of terms, but to offer conceptual clarification in order to ensure coherence.

To begin, race as an object of study within the social sciences is understood to be a social construction, both discursive and inscribed in practices (institutional, economic, cultural). Racial categorization is based on the conviction that the basis of (imagined) alterity differentiating human groups is not (solely) social, but (equally) natural.[6] From this perspective, the question of race is not an analytical category within the social sciences, nor even the life sciences, but a grouping of statements and political norms taken into account by the former.

Next, it's clear that we are dealing with racial categorization in political discourse and institutions from the moment that the following idea is expressed or implied: the moral or social characteristics of persons and communities are transmitted from generation to generation through fluids (blood, sperm, milk) or bodily tissue. This concept explains why individuals remain attached to the behaviors and beliefs rooted in their bodies, even after adopting foreign or imposed moral or social characteristics. Belief in physiological transmission has both literal expressions (blood actually transfers inherited qualities) and more metaphorical ones (for example, the vague understanding of heritage wherein the physical qualities and the social effects of belonging to a specific lineage merge). These do not represent two alternative branches, and even less so two successive phases, of racial ideology. In every circumstance, these types of discourses and institutions deprive the individual of the faculty to not belong to the race to which he or she was born, and the population in question from undergoing any true transformation.[7] Racial thought freezes populations in a time without history and boxes individuals into immutable belonging or affiliation. The fact that the title of Maurice Olender's book, in its original French edition, *Race sans histoire* (race without history) is a derivative of Claude Lévi-Strauss's *Race et histoire* (race and history) shows to what extent racial thought, even when it incorporates more or less historicized arguments, invents invariables and analyzes crossbreeding between populations as phenomena that escape and surpass history.

This definition of racial categorization relies on the importance accorded to the intergenerational transmission of attributes. Racial reasoning is not set in motion by the static examination of a single generation, but rather by anticipation or a retrospective look at the origin of man, and most often by a combination of the two.[8] The racial categories mobilized by actors for political ends cannot therefore be conflated with every form of stigmatization. They retain a certain number of specific characteristics, which were identified in a list by Claude Lévi-Strauss. Their order is worth considering, though that does not mean that any one of the list's components can be eliminated:

As an anthropologist, I am convinced that racist theories are both monstrous and absurd. But by trivializing the notion of racism, applying it this way and that, we empty it

of its meaning and run the risk of producing a result
counter to the one we seek. For what is racism? A specific
doctrine, which can be summed up in four points. One,
there is a correlation between genetic heritage on the one
hand and intellectual aptitudes and moral inclinations on
the other. Two, this heritage, on which these aptitudes and
inclinations depend, is shared by all members of certain
human groups. Three, these groups, called "races," can be
evaluated as a function of the quality of their genetic heritage. Four, these differences authorize the so-called superior "races" to command and exploit the others, and even-
tually destroy them.[9]

Racism cannot be reduced to the doctrine on which it constructs its arguments; however, any form of segregation that
does not rely on such a doctrine can only ever engage racial politics in a metaphorical way.

Finally, insofar as the establishment of pertinent chronol-
ogies is a vital step for historians, it appears necessary to take
a position on the use of the Greek prefix *proto* (as in "protoracism") in historical study. The prefix is used to indicate
the presence of a historical phenomenon that is not yet fully
developed. It is used in several chapters of the reference book
The Origins of Racism in the West,[10] an unsurprising choice
given that the work proposes a long chronology of racism
that begins in Greco-Roman antiquity. Apart from the exceptions that seem to merit use of the term "racism," as indicated
above, the choice to utilize the prefix *proto*, though intended
to contribute a nuance of caution and restraint, only adds to
the confusion. In the example of *The Origins of Racism in the
West*, as no doubt for any other within the historiographical
domain, the prefix *proto* reflects a teleological objective and
inevitably implies a degree of discomfiture. But it does little to

solve the problem at hand and instead tends to further cloud understanding. Of course, there are moments in everyday life when we observe a process in progress whose conclusion or consequences we can easily imagine. And of course, the ability to project into the future is integral to both our actions and thoughts. Therefore rejecting the utility of the prefix *proto* does not mean denying that the prospect of a possible future or outcome can shape actions and choices. However, it's important to distinguish between looking ahead to a possible future or outcome (the future of the present) and looking backward to a fixed future or outcome (the future of the past). The latter concept evokes certainty and refers to an outcome that did indeed take place and that people from the past may have been able to predict but could not know for certain. To speak of ancient or medieval protoracism is equivalent to saying that those periods produced resources (textual, plastic, normative) that other societies were much later able to exploit to their own ends.

But the prefix *proto* implies even more than that. It suggests that a specific Western history deployed sociopolitical and ideological mechanisms that led to, or encouraged, the establishment of racist regimes. Here, as it were, we are dealing with a prospective, not retrospective, genealogy. This position is all the more alarming given that the choice of the classical period (the Greek city-state, the Roman Republic and Empire) reproduces the most traditional model of anchoring the modern Western world in an antiquity from which it was born—in other words, an antiquity already swelling with a modernity it would have been unable to foresee. Criticism of this genealogical progression has been made for some time, notably at the intersections of philosophy, cultural anthropology, and philology. Historians can no longer feign that such criticisms are not relevant to their own understanding of ancient societies.

To conclude, it is important to address racism, or rather the term "racism." We know that the word is a fairly recent addition to the French lexicon. Its first occurrence can be traced to an article by Albert Maybon published in the *Revue blanche* in 1902, in which he denounced the reactionary and chauvinistic character of the Félibrige cultural movement for the revival of the Occitan culture. Aware that he was inventing a neologism, the author had the term "racism" printed in italic characters. According to the *Oxford English Dictionary*, the first printed use in English dates back to the same year. It appears in the proceedings of the twentieth conference of the Friends of the Indian (1902), which met every year on the shores of Lake Mohonk, and which stated that the "association of races and classes is necessary in order to destroy racism and classism." This concurrence inevitably brings to mind the simultaneous appearance of the word "civilization" in 1756 in the Marquis de Mirabeau's treatise *The Friend of Man* and during a lecture given by Adam Ferguson at Edinburgh University.[11] The coincidental occurrence of "racism" simply signifies that the possibility of the term's creation was present within the context of an international intellectual exchange. However, the term's diffusion and propagation would not begin until the 1920s.

In the language of historians, the term "racism" can be employed in place of "racial ideology," in which case it offers little beyond convenience, for example, by allowing the writer to avoid the pitfall of repetition and discard cumbersome expressions like "racial category," "racial doctrine," and "racial ideology," as well as terms like "race," which lack meaning as an analytical tool in the French language. But the term "racism" may serve an additional purpose besides providing an alternate way to designate racial doctrines, which it has done since the beginning of the twentieth century. It strikes me as more interesting to accord a specific meaning to the word "racism" in order to designate ideologies and institutional practices that prioritize racial distinctions in regards to political action—or that attempt to do so. On the doctrinal level, according to the definition I attribute it, racism establishes a hierarchy of historical causalities that considers racial segregation to be the most fundamental driving force in social and political life. In this respect, it is inappropriate to use the term to acknowledge racial distinctions in societies in which no theorist, nor any political or institutional disposition, would have recognized something other than race, for example divine will or the fate of an empire, as the fundamental driving force in history.

A Turning Point: The Early Modern Western Colonial Expansion

Notwithstanding the limitations highlighted in the previous chapter, the following pages, as the reader will see, are in no way shaped as a general critique of race theories in the Anglophone social sciences. On the contrary, this work draws from those arguments and recognizes the debt owed them. Nonetheless, avoiding the facile generalization of the American example and exclusive reliance on Anglophone publications seems indispensable. In the end, the notion of race as it is used in the American social sciences is both very broad, in the sense that it includes various types of distinctive criteria (notably class and gender), and is all too frequently restricted to contemporary American society. The argumentation laid out in this book digresses somewhat from that model: while the scope is limited to the question of the attribution of phenomena of alterity to nature, my analysis relies on a longer history and a greater diversity of situations.

This book is therefore not meant to challenge existing scholarship on race within the Anglophone social sciences.

For instance, the current chapter relies on a problematic constructed by George M. Fredrickson in *Racism: A Short History*, written at the end of his long career as a researcher studying white supremacy in the United States and South Africa.[12]
Fredrickson theorizes a link between the notion of blood purity in Iberia, used to reject religious converts of Jewish or
Muslim origin, and the behavior and norms engendered by
Europe's colonial ventures, including slavery on a large scale,
and leading up to the racist policies of the southern United
States, Nazism, and apartheid. Like many historians of the
United States and South Africa, Fredrickson had rooted his
historical inquiry uniquely on racism against blacks during the
colonial and especially the postcolonial periods. By his own
admission, Fredrickson's method in his last book was aimed
at remedying a historiographical situation that he describes
in the following way:

> Since the bifurcation of studies of white supremacy and
> anti-semitism that took place after World War II, there
> have been few serious efforts to write histories of racism
> that encompass both the antisemitic and the color-coded
> varieties.[13]

The convergence Fredrickson establishes between practices
of stigmatization and the exclusion of Jews in the late Middle
Ages and during the Renaissance is particularly remarkable.
Indeed, contrary to similar surveys, Fredrickson does not propose a chronological inventory of racialization processes.[14] His
explicit objective consists of linking the "Jewish question" and
the "black question" within the framework of an Atlantic history of medium duration.

Other historians have used the same approach. Take, for
example, Henry Méchoulan's work on blood purity, which analyzes together the stigmatization of Native Americans and

the Jews and Moriscos in Iberian territories.[15] More recently, Adriano Prosperi, a specialist in the Roman Inquisition, outlined his view that fifteenth-century Iberia constitutes a fundamental period in the history of the West in general:[16]

> A quick examination of the volume of studies and debates engendered by the history of Iberian Judaism and its elimination indicates the considerable space the events that occurred in Spain at the end of the fifteenth century would eventually occupy in the historiographical understanding of our contemporary world that emerged from the French Revolution.[17]

Starting with the history of religious institutions from Roman Christianity to the Middle Ages and then to modern times, Prosperi interprets the transition from persecution of Jews to that of converted Jews as a foundational process of racialization:

> Far from doing away with religious hatred, the year 1492, a turning point that definitively ended the Jewish presence in Spain, resulted in its transformation into racial hatred. From that moment on, the hunt for Jewish blood, an ineradicable and secret stain that could remain concealed in anyone's genealogy, would put unending investigations into motion.[18]

This citation requires commentary: the indelible "stain" that the Inquisition was charged with flushing out was not concealed within a household's secrets and hidden practices, but in the branches of its family tree. In other words, the reality—or the realization—of stigma was not based predominantly on reprehensible (i.e., heretical) behaviors but on the intergenerational circulation of suspicious blood. That is precisely why, to cite Adriano Prosperi, investigations into blood purity would be "unending," as would be the ramifications of lineage. The weight of this inquisition, so fixated on defining familial compositions, and which never came to a definitive end, once prompted Brazilian historian Maria Luiza Tucci Carneiro to speak of "institutional racism" in regards to the Iberian sociopolitical system during the colonial era or, if preferred, the Ancien Régime.[19] In a three-part series on the Marrano experience in colonial and contemporary Brazil, Nathan Wachtel concludes that the Inquisition was in the vanguard of political modernity among the Hispanic monarchies and, based on its ability to track descendants of converts throughout the world and over several centuries, operated as the administration of a totalitarian state.[20] Finally, among the authors who recently collaborated with Nikolaus Böttcher, Bernd Hausberger, and Max Hering Torres on a volume published by the Colegio de México on the "burden of blood" in colonial Spanish America, the majority approach the issue of race in these societies as one of their principal sociopolitical and religious dimensions.[21]

Adriano Prosperi's argument relies on an empirical understanding of the history of the processes of transformation of Western societies. Occasionally, studies on the most contemporary situations are preceded, as a principle of methodology or professional courtesy, by a historical summary. Sometimes, this kind of addition can serve as a gesture of cross disciplinary goodwill. However, this friendly deference quite often produces results that are even more regrettable than the total absence of any historical foundation. For example, consider what becomes of the hypothesis of the rupture of 1492, as a historiographical proposal and as formulated by Prosperi, a historian, in the hands of other authors. In their authoritative work on race scholarship, sociologists Michael Omi and Howard Winant describe the historicity of racial segregations in the West in the following terms:

Race consciousness, and its articulation in theories of race, is largely a modern phenomenon. When European explorers in the New World "discovered" people who looked different than themselves, these "natives" challenged then existing conceptions of the origins of the human species, and raised disturbing questions as to whether all could be considered in the same "family of man." Religious debates flared over the attempt to reconcile the Bible with the existence of "racially distinct" people.[22]

The rupture of 1492 is thus situated in a position of absolute historical antecedence. According to this theory, racial interpretation of differences was the product of contact by Europeans with Native American populations, of whom they had never heard, and the colonial activities that followed. The stupefaction of the former group didn't arise from an unprecedented experience (just barely evoked by the choice of the expression "the New World"), but rather from the fact that the natives were physically different.

Furthermore, their existence was absent from biblical texts. This theory prompts at least three objections from a historical perspective. First, belief in the intergenerational and physical transmission of infamy or stigma was present in a medieval society that had not yet undertaken transcontinental maritime expansion.[23] Next, experiences with visible physiological alterity date further back as well, if one recalls that black Africans were a visual reality present or represented throughout the long history of relations between the European continent and the Mediterranean region.[24] Finally, other societies with no connection to the New World, either geographically or in their relationships with Europe, starting with those in southern and eastern Asia, had an impact on anthropology and biblical chronology as thunderous as that of Native American populations.[25]

While scholars in other fields have dramatically misinterpreted historical work on the 1492 turning point, a growing number of historians themselves are doing important work in this area. In his recent book *Racisms: From the Crusades to the Twentieth Century*, the historian Francisco Bethencourt like Prosperi and others mentioned suggests situating the formation of racial categories in the Western Christian world in a specific era (between the end of the Middle Ages and the Renaissance) and in specific territories (the Iberian Peninsula):

Although pogroms, expulsions, and the enslavement of Jews and Muslims had been practiced during the Crusades and as a result of conquest, it was the last centuries of the Middle Ages, from the thirteenth to the fifteenth century, that saw the systematic segregation, violent conversion, and exclusion of communities of a different religious origin in Latin Christian areas. Prejudices against Jews and Muslims based on religious differences became linked to the idea of descent. These two religious communities also became connected in Latin ecclesiastical legislation in a practical process of discrimination and segregation that lumped them together as the "enemy within." Both communities were subjected to procedures of spatial, social, and professional segregation, sometimes even after they converted to Christianity. The notion of purity of blood became particularly rooted in Iberia, where it was used to discriminate against and segregate converted Jews and Muslims, showing how religion and ethnic descent had become entangled. This was the crucial case of racism in this period, since it contradicted the universalist ideal of the Christian Church, based on equality among believers from different ethnic origins. Finally, prejudice against black people is documented in the Mediterranean area from classical antiquity onward. Medieval Islamic and Christian writers renewed it, anticipating widespread scorn triggered by the increase of slave trade from Africa to Europe and then to America in the following centuries.[26]

In contrast to Fredrickson, Prosperi, and Bethencourt, another historian, James Sweet, doesn't mention the subject of converted Jews and Muslims (in an article nonetheless entitled "The Iberian Roots of American Racist Thought") even as he attempts to trace the history of the formation of racial categories in the Western world back to the fifteenth century, beginning with the experience of Iberian societies.[27] This omission appears doubly paradoxical as not only does Sweet's study focus on Hispano-Portuguese roots, but it also proposes a chronology that corresponds to the first decades of the sixteenth century, in other words an era of mounting persecution and discrimination against families of Jewish origin, as well as Moriscos, in the kingdoms of Castile, Aragon, and Portugal. Sweet's objective consists of tracking the first manifestations of segregation against blacks in the United States, but he neglects to note the parallel between discrimination against Jews and Moriscos and discrimination against blacks.

An intellectual effort to link different sources of racialization is, however, the most fruitful option. Philosopher and legal expert Eric Voegelin hinted as much in his critical analysis of the concept of race, published in 1933 in Vienna:

> Every race must have a counterrace or antirace, which is, in fact, what the Jews have occasionally been called. Which group of the population functions as the counterrace depends on the prevailing population structure of the territory in which the race idea gains ground as well as on external circumstances. In the United States the race idea chiefly has *two* counterraces: the Negroes and the

immigrants from southern and eastern Europe. . . . In Europe today, this definition of race through its counterrace takes place in its broadest sphere through the counterimage of the Jews.[28]

This excerpt from Voegelin's treatise is in keeping with the rest of the passage. Yet, perhaps not entirely deliberately, three periods are emphasized: the long history of the formation of European anti-Semitism, racism in the United States against the descendants of slaves and immigrants who were neither British nor northern European, and finally, anti-Semitism under the Third Reich. A drive begins in Europe, is fulfilled in America, and returns to Europe in the form of the racial state: a spatial mise-en-scène and a temporal succession to capture our scientific imagination. It is by tracing racist thought back to its European origins that philosophers like Voegelin, and historians today, can find the common thread linking the history of anti-Semitism since the early modern era and the racism against blacks in America. The recent essay by law professor James Q. Whitman on the influence of US segregationist racism in the definition of Nuremberg (1935) Nazi laws has provided a demonstration of how the transatlantic loop of racism between Europe and America has been closed.[29]

It's important to note that none of the authors cited above propose a linear and teleological history of the West that would have inevitably led to the tragedy of the Holocaust. It goes without saying that the genocide of Jews and Gypsies by the Nazi regime occupies an important position in the mind and perhaps in memory. Yet liberating ourselves from this moral tug is essential to avoid reducing Western history to a time line of unavoidable catastrophe, which runs contrary to the historian's critical reasoning. Moreover, it is out of the question to assert that anti-Semitism and negrophobia in the early modern era conform to the same logic and follow the same processes as contemporary—and paroxysmal—forms of racist policies. The cautious approach adopted by the historians previously cited echoes that of Yosef Yerushalmi, when he carefully compares early modern Iberian anti-Semitism with modern German anti-Semitism.[30] By not confusing different epochs in a flat narrative without historical depth, we can find ways to identify racial policies that largely predate our modern era. To be fully persuasive, scholarship on the long history of the formation of racial categories must be subjected to verification of two criteria: no anachronisms and no teleological arguments. These two parameters constitute the elementary stage of intellectual verification within the field of history. As concerns us, they also facilitate study of race over a long duration, without conflating eras, societies, or regions around the world and without ruling out the possibilities of comparison.[31] Furthermore, thanks to those criteria, we are liberated from attempts to suppress our horror in the face of contemporary disasters—an unrealistic endeavor in any case—and our disgust at everyday manifestations of racism—which would constitute an artificial and vain effort indeed. By using the methodology of good historical research, we can avoid tinting the past through the lens of our contemporary biases, no matter how ingrained these contemporary views may be. What complicates the work of historians is that it is not enough to say that the processes of the past have nothing in common with contemporary processes: that would be lazy and too easy. The real difficulty is to determine the exact measure of what is common and what is distinct in the different periods.

The line of reasoning in this work does not echo the conclusions of the numerous studies offering an inventory of racial, raciological, racist, and eugenic doctrines, which self-identify as such, beginning in the second half of the nineteenth century, by authors including André Pichot and Pierre-André Taguieff, among many others. In effect, the political and social historical agenda presented here approaches the problem differently. On the one hand, it identifies racial statutes even, and perhaps especially, when they do not identify themselves as such. On the other, it examines the impact of political regulation of alterity or processes of racialization of individuals and whole communities on social, cultural, and intellectual levels, rather than the other way around.

By avoiding teleology and anachronism, historical inquiry can isolate common processes across societies that have contributed to the formation of racial categories in different political contexts. The history of these processes describes the ways by which populations were assigned distinct identities (alterity) understood as natural (biological) differences. A panoramic look at a large group of societies allows us to sketch a provisional typology of these processes. In Europe, Africa, Asia, and the Americas, the naturalization of statutory inferiority rests on three main oppositions: association with infamous professions as opposed to honorable professions and occupations; the condition of descendants of conquered and vanquished populations as opposed to that of descendants of victorious conquerors; and belonging to a religiously suspicious community as opposed to communion in dominant religious orthodoxy. For each of these great types of cleavages, one finds that the negative reputation, whose origin is of course always social, ends up becoming a constitutive element of the nature of persons and communities discriminated against. Therefore, the history of racial categories deals with a specific subcategory of a much larger category—*alterity*—that, in its turn, belongs to the arsenal of political domination. Within the social sciences, the subject of alterity is as impossible to conceptualize as that of xenophobia, owing notably to its overly generic nature. Because it is based on a principle of separation, the production of alterity reflects a relational dynamic. It results from an action by which one segment of one society describes collective differences, attributes them to other segments of society, and maintains their generally high degree of immutability. Producing alterity often serves to legitimize a policy of subjugation, but it can also prove indifferent to the construction of a sociopolitical balance of power. Today, in the context of the development of a historiography increasingly focused on imperial and colonial dynamics, emphasis is placed more often on the links between the creation of alterity and strategies of domination.[32] That said, we cannot dismiss the possibility that the losers of colonial confrontations also produced discourse about alterity in order to characterize their dominators or any other social segment. The position of victim does not insulate any society, group, or individual from the temptation of defining the alterity of those they consider different from themselves. This faculty is restored to them by a history and anthropology careful to reconstruct the capacity of dominated actors to exist and act other than under the command of their dominators or as passive objects of persecution—with agency, in other words. When analyses of power relations conducted within the social sciences take into account the political faculties of dominated groups, their capacity also to create dynamics of hermetic identities and to marginalize others becomes apparent. In this broad context, and among works dedicated to the history of diasporas, some researchers reconstruct the processes of identity formation of isolated groups and highlight the multidimensional character of collective belonging, including the temptation of forming ghettos.[33]

The work of historians is shaped by the nature of their source documents. Researchers are therefore inevitably guided by the fact that the writing and images produced by dominant groups, and which have been conserved until now, are more abundant and extensive than those created by groups lower in the social hierarchy, which rarely benefited from the same level of attention to preservation. Consequently, it's very tempting to focus historical inquiry not on the phenomena described in these sources, but on the social practices by which dominant groups used their mastery of writing to define norms and condemn deviations. This research angle is by nature critical and reflexive. It attempts to counterbalance the asymmetric character of available documentation in order to identify and understand social relations in ancient societies.[34] Within mechanisms of inherited stigmatization during the late Middle Ages, the segments of societies designated as "different" in chronicles, moral tracts, and legal texts, in comparison to a dominant model, represented the vast majority of the population: women, poor farmers, manual laborers, vagrants, illegitimate children, sorcerers, lunatics, lepers, gypsies, Cagots, Jews, slaves, minority linguistic groups, heretics, homosexuals, and so on.[35] One can speculate that in imperial and colonial frameworks, the demographic weight of the dominant group was even smaller than it was within European societies. As a result, the proportion of inhabitants in a colonial territory considered to be divergent from the dominant model must have been much larger than the equivalent in Europe. Lists of subjugated groups implicitly read as definitions, which we can situate in comparison to Erving Goffman's attempt to isolate the characteristics of individuals free of all stigma:

> In an important sense, there is only one complete unblushing male in America: a young, married, white, urban, northern, heterosexual Protestant father of college education, fully employed, of good complexion, weight, and height, and a recent record in sports.[36]

Unlike historians—who, when faced with the paucity of historical sources from the so-called losers' or subalterns' perspective, confront one of the cruelest limits of their profession—sociologists and ethnologists can hope to see the other side of the equation and measure to what extent the victims of the kind of categorization cited above internalize the inferiority attributed to them, as well as to what extent they are capable of rejecting it. For the most part, historical sources reinforce the effects of domination thanks to the concentration of written expression among social categories that explain and diffuse ideology of their superiority. From this perspective, historians' reliance on the work of sociologists and ethnologists is both indispensable and liberating. While historians have much to contribute to the study of race, and close attention to history can help scholars avoid misconceptions such as assuming a link must exists between race and skin color, other disciplines have important roles to play in helping us form a clearer understanding of race.

Xenophobia, which is not intrinsically attached to a framework of domination, presents a different, though equally frustrating, problem. Fear or rejection of the other is a phenomenon that can be identified in any location, during any time period, and, most importantly when it comes to methodology, at any scale. Reciprocal grievances can manifest at every possible level and can disappear at another scale of observation: two (or more) neighborhoods in a village, two villages in the same valley, two countries in the same region, two regions of the same kingdom, kingdom versus kingdom. Furthermore, contrary to the study of alterity that, at the least, assumes that collective actors have the capacity to provide substance to identity and alterity, for themselves and for those from whom they want to distinguish themselves, xenophobia does not presuppose any particular social capacity. Therefore, it presents an impossible object of study for historians.

Stigmatization and Racial Ideologies

In the course of study of racial categories, it is imperative to examine other phenomena of stigmatization: notions of religious infidelity; a substandard or inadequate stage of development according to a vision of the progress humanity is meant to achieve; unacceptable social behaviors (which can include sexuality, clothing choice or nudity, alcoholism, and so on); objects of moral condemnation; class and work relationships; the shame attached to certain professions; the negative effects of territorial segregation that are understood as having caused themselves; and so on. The best studies in this domain rely on a blend of two historiographical styles: the analysis of processes of stigmatization as they occurred, in empirical terms, in Europe and the colonies during the Ancien Régime; and the study of ideological resources mobilized in order to anchor politics of social differentiation on racial prejudice.

The first approach focuses on practices of spatial segregation, cultural distinction (clothing, food, beliefs, sexual and matrimonial mores, access to reading and writing), religious persecution (by Europeans in relation to non-Europeans, and between Europeans), and legal and statutory inferiorization (slaves, dependents, the exploited). These mechanisms deployed to the detriment of populations colonized and deported from Africa, including plantation and even mining slave labor, also served to confine low-ranking Europeans to politically inferior situations. In this respect, it is important to integrate the ways the question of the savage, barbarian, civilized, or advanced character of the societies impacted by colonialism was formulated (and resolved) between the Renaissance and the Enlightenment. The perception of alterity in a colonial context could manifest as a radical rejection of the vanquished and conquered populations if, for example, Europeans perceived the image of a demonic world in a territory or a population they encountered.[37] This line of inquiry must also take into account the existence of "internal Indias," according to the expression found in the correspondence of missionaries, meaning the persistence within Europe itself of collective behaviors (heterodox beliefs, uncontrolled celebrations, stigmatized mores, superstitions) that, according to dominant groups, needed to be repressed and corrected through the effects of preaching and even missionary work.[38]

During the Ancien Régime, jurists, moralists, and various educated persons produced social and institutional descriptions in the form of nomenclatures. Taking advantage of the vast quantity of texts, regulations, and provisions produced as a result of the desire to distinguish social groups, António Manuel Hespanha recently published a book analyzing the attribution of collective weakness and inferiority in the early modern era.[39] The concerned groups are children, women, madmen and those of diminished responsibility, rural dwellers, nomads, savages, and barbarians. Hespanha's analysis emphasizes the extreme rigidity of these social and cultural discriminations. The prevailing political and religious ideology throughout the Ancien Régime, up to the challenge presented by the Enlightenment to the Old World at least, rests on the conviction that the order that organizes human societies must, like the order of nature, remain unchanged. Hence, the immutability of status was a result of the ideological advantage accorded to a fixed order confronted with any indetermination. Even though the colonial dimension of this model is taken into account, via pages on the subject of slavery, Hespanha's study of the categorization of inferior groups does not mobilize the category of race, not because the author denies the relevance of studies on the existence of raciological reasoning in ancient societies, but rather because that is not his primary target.

From the point of view that concerns us, however, Hespanha's approach suggests, somewhat by omission, that research on racial categories cannot be conflated with the general study of practices of domination and even less so be substituted for them. It is worth repeating, though undoubtedly obvious, that racial discrimination is a valuable political resource in the complex arsenal of instruments of domination within a much more extensive collection of resources.

The second approach pays particular attention to the long-denigrated notion of ideology and aims to go beyond an inventory, which has been produced countless times, of the stereotypes found in the texts and images that remain from the Ancien Régime. It therefore does not consist of translating or reproducing the series of clichés that have been saddled on various peoples by a large number of voyagers, real or armchair, pamphletists, and cartographers. When the historical approach is limited to collecting a succession of these kinds of more or less conventional representations, the critical information obtained remains feeble. Historical investigations of ideological systems are far more demanding. They involve reconstructing social configurations and political practices by which the natural inferiority of dominated groups acts as a framework for individual and collective action, which can be shared by dominator and dominated alike. From this perspective, Giuliano Gliozzi's excellent book about the anthropology that accompanied European expansion until the modern era, as a colonial ideology, remains an example of coherence.[40] In the same fashion, Jennifer Morgan, in her work on the link between racialized descriptions of Native Americans and Africans, emphasizes a foreign type of femininity. Morgan's research on the production of a system of ethnicized and gendered domination relates to what she calls "racial ideology."[41]

If we examine, for example, the various ways to explain the links between slavery and racial thinking, historiography has favored two models. Either the system of slave labor used on plantations necessitated a set of ad hoc beliefs whose function was to justify the fate reserved for slaves by describing their nature as inferior and even inhuman or cursed by the never-ending ramifications of Noah's curse on his son Ham and his grandson Canaan. Or Europe's long heritage of persecution of stigmatized minorities and thirst for stereotypes rendered the enslavement of Native Americans and blacks, among other groups, morally admissible.

In an article that remains a major reference in the field, Barbara Jeanne Fields ironizes the tendency to favor a cultural approach to links between slavery and racial doctrine in terms that serve as a warning:

> Probably a majority of American historians think of slavery in the United States as primarily a system of race relations—as though the chief business of slavery were the production of white supremacy rather than the production of cotton, sugar, rice and tobacco. . . . If the slaveholders had produced white supremacy without producing cotton, their class would have perished in short order.[42]

Today, the theme of "racialization" within imperial and colonial frameworks eliminates the need to choose between a focus on racial prejudice and one on slavery and colonial domination, thanks to a perspective that analyzes social domination as the fruit of dynamic processes and not as the result of the application of legal norms or market methods defined independently of the reality of power relations in each place and at different times.[43] Each approach contributes to the other, thereby creating common ground for current-day historiography.

Using the study of ideologies of domination as a jumping-off point thus ensures that the historian does not isolate the mobilization of racial arguments at the end of the early modern/colonial era from the rest of the historical analysis of social relationships. This approach similarly does away with the notion that racial issues, identified as early as the late Middle Ages, absorbed all other processes of the sociogenesis of alterity. Ania Loomba underscores this in the introduction to her work on race in Shakespeare's theater:

> The rise of modern racism is often seen in terms of a shift from a cultural (and more benign) to a more biological (and inflexible) view of racial difference. But although the biological understanding of race made it more pernicious, we should be wary of positing a simple opposition between nature and culture or suggesting that a "cultural" understanding of race is somehow benign and flexible. In fact, what we call "race" and what we call "culture" cannot be readily separated, especially during the early modern period when a "people's inferior culture implied a biologically inferior people."[44]

Between the end of the medieval period and the revolutionary era in Europe and the colonies, the rationale used to maintain dominated groups in an inferior position was organized around four primary categories.

The oldest is without a doubt the campaign against obstinate religious misinterpretation (or error) in regards to the Creator and the revealed truths. Jews, Muslims and other infidels, Cathars, pagans with hardened hearts, and heretics of a perverted Christianity all had to be kept at a distance, even if missionary outreach was possible. This also applied to Jews who had converted to Christianity and were nonetheless suspected of maintaining their attachment to the outdated, and thus erroneous, law of Moses. In his own terms, Max Hering Torres defines "racist anti-Judaism" as an "oxymoron" that has molded Iberian societies since the dawn of the modern era.[45] In the case of the America of conquistadors and missions, the desire to convert others was at odds with the sobering realization that it was a hopeless endeavor. This early disenchantment took root in the minds of Europeans, particularly the clergy, beginning in the fifteen century in regards to the conversion of Jews and Muslims, and during the sixteenth century in regards to evangelized Native Americans. This is undoubtedly one of the first manifestations of the quandaries of evolutionism, this way of conceiving that non-European societies are destined, in a single historical process, to align themselves with the way Christian Europe defines the higher values of civilization.[46]

Religious failure, or the suspicion of it, fueled the belief that certain populations lacked the ability to follow—in other words, they were born incapable of following—a path that would lead them to a fully civilized system. This is the second major aspect of the rationale of domination, and it lies at the heart of any historical investigation on the attribution of savagery or barbarism to, for example, the Irish, Native Americans, or Africans. This belief led to the emergence of a theory centered on a backwardness that could be corrected only by a very slow process of transformation, in stark contrast to the immediacy of baptism or the administration of the sacraments. Captivity and forced labor would obtain results that sacraments and divine grace visibly couldn't. It was in the long-term, then, that forced labor and enslavement would offer barbarians, or at least their descendants, a chance to take their first steps beyond savagery.[47]

The third ideological category worth exploring in regards to the rationale of domination is the attribution of abnormal femininity to men belonging to segregated groups, a way of expressing contempt. Gender distinctions, believed clear in the dominant society, are reputed to be poorly defined in certain dominated societies. One of the most famous Western examples is the claim that Jewish men menstruated.[48] This stigma had the advantage of inscribing Jewish transgression into a corporal difference even though it was rendered invisible by clothing that concealed the shameful secret. The other famous case relates to the natives of America whose weak pilosity was interpreted as the sign of degeneration through feminization, to the point that several authors asserted that male Native Americans had the ability to breastfeed their children.[49]

Perhaps the most lasting element of this ideological complex is the animality attributed to men from stigmatized groups. The imaginary populations found in accounts, etchings, and geographical maps from the late Middle Ages display a mix of human and animal traits. Monopod figures stand alongside men with dog heads or covered with fur from head to toe, for example. Some of Hieronymus Bosch's most famous paintings bear witness to the persistence of images of animalized men and humanized things in the mid-sixteenth century.[50] In the seventeenth century, as anatomy lessons became commonplace, at least in Protestant countries, Edward Tyson's research on a chimpanzee skeleton, wrongly identified as that of an orangutan, attempted to show the similarity between great apes and Africans.[51] Removing blacks from a shared humanity nourished a polygenic conception of man's presence on Earth. Starting in the eighteenth century, anatomical drawings were used to show the difference between specific types of men and an ideal aesthetical model (the Apollo Belvedere) in contrast to major natural history publications.[52] At the same time, the question of anatomical proximity to primates or other animals spanned the colonial Ancien Régime and haunted the first decades of postrevolutionary societies.[53]

These four themes do not appear at all times or in all regions of Europe, its empires, and its colonies. But they most often emerge in combination. As a result, in order to understand the racial ideology in all its expressions, historians of the subject must have three types of knowledge available: the political processes that form societies, the development of the natural sciences, and finally art history and aesthetic sensibilities. If a single specialty is prioritized, the historian's reasoning could prove false. At one extreme, he or she risks obtaining a perfect equivalence between socioeconomic domination and racial inferiorization, in which case any specificities of racial prejudice related to other sources of domination would be dismissed. At the other extreme, the historian can settle for producing a catalog of textual and plastic representations of stigmatized populations. But neither of these two models allows for an understanding of the effectiveness and hold of racial ideology on its champions and designated victims during each of the historical periods under consideration. Historians must develop the tools to study the ideology beneath racial distinctions, and they must place racialization within the context of larger processes of stigmatization.

Race and Naturalization of Conflicts

The definition of racism proposed earlier—the idea of an intergenerational and physiological transmission of moral characteristics—inscribes racial policies into the category of discrimination based on the attribution of natural traits (congenital, hereditary), and as a result it confines racism and race to the realm of biological fictions. Ethnic or religious minorities and descendants of lineages that are infamous (professionally or otherwise) are not the only categories of people who are subjected to a process of racialization.

Let's focus, as an example that today seems hard to believe, on one country, Spain, in the twentieth century, when the notion of racial purity appeared to be have been discredited, even within the most conservative circles. The social sciences emerging in Spain at that time were clearly echoes of the fields of physical anthropology and raciology found in other European countries.[54] Historical awareness of the multiplicity of invasions and migrations that formed the Spanish population was being eclipsed, though not forgotten, by Catholic universalism and the colonial history of Hispanity. Nonetheless, the repressive Francoist regime borrowed the Nazis' racist model during the Spanish Civil War and in the wake of the nationalists' victory. Granted, pro-Franco Spanish doctors did not give in to the temptation of eugenics in its most coercive (forced sterilizations, abortions) or criminal (executions) forms out of respect for Catholic principles. But this divergence from practices present in other contemporary societies does not signify that belief in the racial transmission of traits, good or bad, was absent from the official ideology and repressive practices that emerged in Spain in the 1940s.[55] The famous psychiatrist Antonio Vallejo Nágera, who distinguished himself by classifying Marxist affiliation as a mental pathology, was a prolific spokesman of National Catholicism–inspired political hygienism.[56] His personal application of eugenics was restricted to limiting Communist or Republican female prisoners to one hour of daily contact with their newborn infants in order to spare the children the effects of harmful contamination.

But even before the Francoist camps and prisons filled with political prisoners, Vallejo Nágera had produced an ambiguous doctrine that became part of the long history of the formation of the Spanish consciousness. Like many past and even current historians, the psychiatrist regarded the question of blood purity in his Spanish society as restricted to the spiritual domain, with no strong racial signification:

> Racist attitudes were always latent in Spain, as shown by records from earlier centuries on the blood purity necessary to hold public office or belong to craft guilds. It is true that blood purity referred primarily to Jewish or Moorish origins, but it was aimed at reinforcing religious purity. A stranger who assimilated the spirit of Hispanity and Hispanic culture metamorphosed into an exalted patriot and Hispanophile, joyfully integrating into our race.[57]

According to Nágera's 1937 text, the Spanish population could not claim an advantageous position in the hierarchies of peoples, as concerns the perspective of Gobineau-esque criteria for purity or those established by Camper on facial angles.[58]

> We the Spanish cannot truly speak about the purity of racial genotypes, without a doubt less so than other peoples, because the different invasions endured by the Peninsula left traces of the most diverse genotypes. The ancient Iberians mixed with Greeks and Romans underwent African, Germanic, Gallic, and even Nordic invasions, the result being a people subjected to countless civilizational influences and interbreeding of various genotypes. . . . Skin color should be accorded importance, because what we call race is not constituted exclusively by biological characteristics that can be transmitted by germ plasm, but by those that are reflections of the mind, as well as of thought and language.[59]

In fact, the Spanish psychiatrist's reflections in 1937 correspond to a tradition that was rather recent at the time—the exaltation of the Hispanic *raza* on both sides of the Atlantic within reactionary circles. Within Spain, and to an even lesser degree in Latin America, the Hispanic *raza* couldn't claim the same level of Aryan or Nordic racial purity as was expressed in German, Anglophone, or Scandinavian societies. Fantasies of Hispanic identity therefore coalesced around an idealized or spiritualized notion of race. Nevertheless, a strictly genealogical and racial line of thought was still present. In 1938, Vallejo Nágera wrote about the internal enemy within Spain at the time, reviving in the process significantly older notions of the exterior and menacing character of religious minorities in Spain in the late Middle Ages:

> Today, as during the Reconquista, we, the Hispano-Romano-Goths, are fighting against the Judeo-Moors. The pure racial trunk versus the bastard. . . . The Spanish Marxist racial trunk is Judeo-Moor, a mix of blood that distinguishes it psychologically from the foreign Marxist, the pure Semite.[60]

It is tempting to view these remarks as simply metaphorical or reflective of a shift in meaning. Indeed, perhaps the language used by Nágera doesn't merit further consideration. Nevertheless, it's interesting to note that the excerpt above relies on a systematic and racialized interpretation of continuous Spanish history beginning with the elimination of Jewish and Muslim societies from Spain and including the civil war. And if a common thread exists from one sequence to another, then we are meant to understand that the conversion of Jews and Muslims was a failure, not because the infidels held on to prohibited beliefs and rites, but because their "ancestral psychology" could not be changed:

> The conversion of those called Marranos had been faked, for convenience, to adapt to circumstances. . . . The

submission in the Christian Jordan did not change the genius of their race, did not transform the ancestral sionite
[*sic*] psychology, his typical avarice, his taste for lies, phi-
listinism, and malice. . . . And when the revolution came
under cover of the republic, the *converso* clearly displayed
his aims, he undid the vital knots of Christian life, he
murdered, he stole, he raped and committed all kinds of
horrors.[61]

The vision of a revolting populace as a barbarian invasion
is a common theme in conservative and reactionary political
writing throughout the nineteenth century. Similar, and more
intensely racialized, overtones can be found within the context
of the Spanish Civil War:

Take a careful look of the color of those yelling out. There
are not many fair-haired among them. Observe the hint of
the Oriental, the Berber in the shuffling crowd. When all is
said and done . . . this strikes me . . . as a new episode of the
conspiracy of muddled races against the Gothic nobility.[62]

The political prophylaxis of the Francoist camp is particularly interesting in terms of the arguments used. For example,
Nágera emphasizes a more spiritual than racial character of
the pure, legitimate Hispanic identity, only to one year later
describe the political enemy using Jewish or Moorish traits
whose inherent malice cannot be eliminated by the sacrament
of baptism. It's clear that the lack of a strong biological argument does not limit the resurgence of the notion that social,
political, or cultural characteristics are inherited naturally.

In the definition of a racially based political argument I provided earlier, I confine the notion of race to a political concept
based on a biologizing ideology, concerning traits that are inherited through blood or other bodily substances, that is hardly

ever expressed anymore, at least not explicitly, in twenty-first-century European society. That such ideas are rarely articulated today does not mean that they are confined to the past, as shown above. But disregarding the potential resurgence of such racial thinking, I am not claiming that any notion of "race" and "racism" has no validity in contemporary society, or that, as many in France would hold, we should not employ such notions in public policy or the social sciences. While I am presenting a limited, historical definition of race, it is necessary that the term be used in a broader sense when applied to society today.[63] Over the past thirty years in the United States, militant and scholarly arguments have emphasized the negative consequences of color blindness, in other words the refusal to consider and see racialized differences, on attempts to establish programs to support minorities. In the first issue of the social sciences publication *Race and Society*, Ronald Taylor established its mission as the imperative to critique indifference to racial difference, a stance that claims to be a method to erase distinctions but that in reality weakens attempts to combat discrimination:

> Calls for the elimination of race as a social category [may] appear progressive against a backdrop of racist discursive practices that characterize contemporary American society. Yet some scholars regard such calls as premature if not misguided, because they are predicated on the false premise that discrediting the term will neutralize its social effects. Based on well-intentioned and ulterior motivations, both liberals and conservatives have embraced the ideology of "color blindness." For liberals, the achievement of equality is realized by the removal of race categories across society and their eradication as sources of identification and analysis. For some conservatives, the rhetoric of color blindness has been appropriated to justify attacks

on social policies and programs perceived to be dispropor-
tionately beneficial to racial minorities, and to relegate the
race concept and the phenomenon of racism to the margins
of political and cultural discourse. In problematizing race,
some right-wing conservatives have sought, ultimately, to
preserve racism.[64]

Granted, this debate is a political one, but it's clearly relevant to researchers in the fields of sociology, demography,
geography, law, and others. In France, within scientific, leg-
islative, and executive spheres, the perpetuation of aphasia in
regards to race results from different series of proposals.

The principal proposal is that cultural markers should not
be taken under consideration by the social sciences, because
to do so is to substitute fantasies or illusions of identity for
objective data. Information that may be useful in determining public policies—social analyses that integrate cultural
variables—are often suspected of wanting to disarm socioeconomic class struggles. The focus on socioeconomic factors,
instead of cultural factors, prompts lawmakers and the public
to look at more or less community-wide behaviors, regardless of whether these behaviors have been passed down or recently created, and whether they are spontaneous or induced
by observed forms of ghettoization, to avoid confronting the
ultimate causality of tensions underlying unequal income distribution. The flaw in taking cultural markers under consideration, or merely recording the geographic origins of individuals in regions marked by intensive population movements,
lies in its substitution of fantasies or illusions of identity for
objective data. The refusal to consider the racial dimensions of
social relations ultimately serves to ensure the elimination of
all forms of culturalism from social science research. In reality
it is clear that targeted manifestations of xenophobia exist in

our societies, which for convenience we qualify as racist. The persistence of racism suggests that we have every reason to question voluntary blindness to the cultural dimension of unilateral or reciprocal antipathy and discrimination present in our societies.

From the point of view of the social sciences, the culturalist approach seems like it should be a sufficient response to the accusation of spreading subtle forms of evolutionism, albeit unknowingly, or, in other words, spreading a European ethnocentric ideology. The debate the French president Nicolas Sarkozy hoped to launch to define nationally what French identity looked like was a total failure. At the least, it offered those who opposed the concept of identity itself the opportunity to gain the largest audience possible for their arguments. Philosopher Michel Serres, for example, voiced his objection to the type of discussion then being proposed by the State. In the simplest terms, Serres demonstrated the imperceptible nature of identity on both the national and the individual (or a small community or group) scale.[65] He pleaded for another, far more pertinent, descriptor of one's position in society: belonging, or rather senses of belonging. Whereas any study or investigation faced with an exclusive or plural identity must confront the unresolvable difficulty of distinguishing between an objective analysis of aspects of their identity and their own subjective sense of identity, an individual's sense(s) of belonging are situated entirely on the side of his or her own choice, in other words accepted subjectivity.[66] Research on cultural affiliation or belonging, and its religious, linguistic, and aesthetic dimensions, aims to describe solidarity-inducing phenomena of collective adhesion, while in no way diminishing individuals' capacity to emancipate themselves from said identity or modify it in accordance with personal choice.

Therefore, by limiting the scope of historical analysis of racial categories to those that explicitly rely on a natural or biological foundation for observed differences, I am not reinforcing French aphasia toward race. Of course, racism does exist without race.[67] Collective discrimination against social groups distinguishable by a shared origin exists. Communities within which behaviors are not all identical exist. All this to say that the loose meaning of the idea of race, as it is expressed in the Anglophone social sciences, is acceptable. It suffices to import and utilize it to analyze the perpetuation of social inequalities in European countries. That, however, is not the object of the study that I am proposing.

Scientific Racism or Nationalist Delirium?

The expression "scientific racism," most commonly employed as a chronological marker to distinguish an era of naive and incoherent racism from a subsequent era of fully developed and systematic racism, warrants commentary. There are three persuasive arguments why the expression should be abandoned in writing about history.

First, the notion of "scientific racism" conflates methods used to identify unique phenotypic and physiological traits in individuals and groups—like the legitimate use of anthropometry, for example, in the health record booklets provided by the French public health system to monitor children's growth—with the type of distorted moral, social, or political inferences made about such measures for ideological purposes by racist thinkers. The fact that proponents of racist rationales record phenotypic and physiological data methodically and with precision does not confer any particular scientific dignity on these proponents of racist rationales, given that their intellectual approach falls entirely within the sphere of political propaganda.

The second, more empirical argument stems from consideration of the distinct content attributed to "scientific racism" as a contribution to modernity in comparison to archaic forms of racism. Take, for example, a definition of scientific racism as a marker of a chronological break in a study of the historical relationship between psychology and racial distinctions. Graham Richards highlights two series of characteristics that he judges to be unique to the "scientific" phase of Western racism:

> Scientific Racism intensified the conflation of the biological and the cultural as biological level explanations came to be considered more fundamentally "scientific." Cultural traits, good and bad, were interpreted as direct expressions of innate racial character, a message seductively packaged in several ways, one being the constant invocation of physiological differences allegedly discovered by trustworthy doctors and anatomists. Adopting European anatomy and physiology as the norm, any deviation became quasi-pathological and described accordingly. Secondly the growing corpus of writings by colonial administrators, missionaries, doctors, traders and travellers provided extensive "authentic" first-hand evidence of the moral, temperamental, intellectual and physical failings of non-Europeans.[68]

The function of the expression "scientific racism" as a chronological marker, according to that definition, is nothing less than obvious. Richards mentions alterity attributed at birth, the description of physiological differences, the tendency to qualify a specific physical feature as an anomaly, and the confidence placed in firsthand and eyewitness accounts. Yet all these elements can be found, to various degrees, in writings that date back to the Renaissance; not one can be defined as specific to the nineteenth century. Therefore, if we were to use the term "scientific racism" to refer to racism of this kind, it must be applied to the entire history of racism that I am examining in this book.

Third, use of the adjective "scientific" in a historiographical argument reinforces the most outdated frameworks in the history of the sciences. It's widely known that the evolutionist discourse that accompanied the birth of "big science," this narrative that selects among the ancient scientific propositions those that have contributed to form the present state of scientific truth, has been the object of profound revisions over the past thirty years.[69] What happens when we situate the age of "scientific racism" at the moment when the experimental life sciences were coming to the forefront during the nineteenth century? We validate the idea that all prior arguments and knowledge related to heredity or climatic variations did not reflect a scientific line of thought. However, whether they called on Hippocrates and Galen, Aristotle and Saint Thomas Aquinas, Pliny and Ptolemy, or even missionary voyagers and their botanist contemporaries from the European expansion to the Renaissance, authors of texts on the natural transmission of human traits believed they were producing scientific conclusions well before the codes of modern experimental science were imposed.[70] Climate theory, analysis of congenital diseases, the first dissections, to cite but a few examples, all preceded the advent of the science to which the notion of "scientific racism" clumsily refers.

When it comes to the critical question of the validity of the hypothesis of heritability of acquired characteristics, where does one find the real science amid the seemingly intractable battle between neo-Lamarckian and neo-Darwinian currents in the late nineteenth century? Was the former always bogged down by its metaphysical aims, even as the latter doubled down on rationality and scientificity after the Darwinian revolution? Anyone observing the controversies that marked the end of the nineteenth century—from a twentieth-century vantage point situated after the development of population genetics, that is—would refuse such a simple qualification of each of the two currents. In an era before nuclear disasters (and epigenetics research) it seemed clear that one must refute the hypothesis of heritability of characteristics acquired during the life of a living being to stay on the side of theoretical rigor and experimental evidence on the scale of intergenerational transmission from individual to individual. The history of a body does not modify the genetic material of said body, or so the argument went. But this argument did not hold in the same way on the scale of populations and in the long term of a great number of generations. This example, which concerns the question of the articulation between hereditary transmission and the history of societies, indicates that at the time when what is termed "scientific racism" is supposed to have triumphed among specialists in hereditary transmission there was no agreement on what was of science and what was metaphysics.

There is no justification for the attribution of the adjective "scientific" to raciology of the second half of the nineteenth century and the first half of the twentieth century. At the most, it signals the tendency of various raciologists to mimic experimental methods. They do so in their social interactions among their contemporaries (correspondences, scholarly organizations, international conferences, journals). It is without a doubt true that these researchers believed that they were producing a kind of science, but neither more nor less so than certain of their distant ancestors, from clerics to astrologists, from surgeons to theologians, who themselves do not merit inclusion into the narrative of the triumph of Western scientific rationality.

Franz Boas, who had no reason to oppose or distrust the statistical results of physical anthropology, wrote that it is not the measurement that makes racial thought, but a noncritical usage of correlation:

We have here one of the numerous cases in which the uncritical use of the concept of correlation leads to unjustifiable conclusions.[71]

The white coat does not transform the racist ideologist into
a man of science. This aligns with the argument that there
were no radically distinct periods of racial thought, since the
Ancien Régime, but rather an evolution of the notion of race
that never was uprooted from its medieval origins, and that
informed racial policies since then onward.

Racism and Universalism

When studying societies between the end of the medieval period and the modern era, one question inevitably emerges: the
incompatibility between Christian ideas of grace and universalism, and prejudice based on people's supposedly unchang-
ing nature. As was discussed in chapter 1, sixteenth-century
Iberian blood purity regulations excluded people with certain
heritage from the efficacy of divine grace. When Spanish Jews
and Muslims converted to Christianity and celebrated bap-
tisms, they were reproached for being unable to sincerely join
the Christian communion. That accusation indicates to what
extent this legal artifact for social regulation was in ideological
contradiction with the religious milieu within which it placed
itself, and which it claimed to serve above all other law.

As highlighted by Ian Hacking, asserting a racial foundation for alterity is all the more necessary when a normative
framework is focused on establishing equality between men:

> The desire of one racial group to dominate, exploit, or en-
> slave another demands legitimacy in societies that, like
> modern Europe and America, are committed to versions
> of egalitarianism. Race sciences were devised to discover

a lot of differences between races that do not follow from the marks of color and structure by which we distinguish them. You do not have to treat people equally, if they are sufficiently different.[72]

Focusing on one period, one region, and one system that are distinct in every way can be illuminating for historical study of the formation of racial categories. For instance, an exhaustive debate arose over programs of radical, societal transformation and collective repression in the Soviet Union, as relates to race. For lack of access to Russian sources, I am relying instead on reflections of those discussions within the Anglophone social sciences, as well as translated dissident literature, as my point of reference.[73] It goes without saying that this detour through Soviet history is not founded on any competence as a researcher. Rather, it simply allows me to reflect, via a different angle, on the antinomy of universal emancipation and racial categorization. Consider four political phenomena: political use of the notion of the wrong class origin; national or ethnic deportations; State and party anti-Semitism after World War II; and in parallel, mass social engineering that used forced labor to foster a new humanity. We can also add the composite and millenarian idea, inspired by Karl Marx and Charles Darwin, according to which certain social categories, having been proven obsolete by the social sciences, would be destined to disappear en masse—meaning men, women, and children if necessary—in order to fulfill the historic law that prophesized their disappearance.

If the debate between specialists of Soviet history is ongoing, it's because the various phenomena cited above are all characterized by a certain degree of ambivalence. If the debate is particularly heated, it's because each of its contributors is understandably operating from the perspective of a comparison between Nazism and bolshevism.

How did the Soviet revolutionary machine's ambivalence toward race manifest itself? Two examples come to mind: the analysis of nationalities policies that favored the officialization of languages unrecognized under the tsarist regime in comparison with large campaigns of ethnic cleansing,[74] and the regime's position on contemporary research on the biology of heredity and eugenics projects. Some accounts maintain that beginning in 1933, motivated by an explicit desire to demarcate itself from Hitlerism, the Soviet regime put an end to an entire series of eugenics-related studies and programs, which had been developed in the USSR as in other contemporary nations.[75] However, this somewhat summary version is contradicted by in-depth study of the history of genetics in the Soviet Union, which reveals the back-and-forths and condemnations and reversals that swept through the Soviet scientific milieu between the 1920s and the 1960s.[76]

Several processes, analyzed in comparison with other societies and other political configurations, also marked the Soviet regime: an obsession with internal pollution, a program of ethnic purification, and aspiration to the creation of a unanimous society. As seen in the preceding pages, this obsession, program, and aspiration were equally apparent in the political, spiritual, and social system of the Iberian monarchies of the Ancien Régime. Returning to Soviet history, which cannot be taken as a whole, the dominant element between the October Revolution and the mid-1930s was the attempt to eliminate classes that were believed to be condemned to disappear according to the prognoses of scientific socialism. This undertaking culminated in the elimination of the Kulaks, who were repressed as a population and not as a group of responsible individuals, that is, "the transformation of 'Kulak' into political category, disconnected from any socioeconomic meaning, but a black stain on repressed individuals."[77] It was preceded by

the ethnic cleansing of the Don Cossacks in 1919, the first attempt at mass repression targeted at communities defined by
an ethnic and social base.[78] During the same period, the "mili-
tarization" of industrial labor and establishment of large infra-
structures created a regime of forced labor that, in the words
of Maxim Gorky (in reference to construction of the White Sea
Canal), would enable prisoners and forced laborers to escape
their "zoological" retardation.[79] This type of "social engineering" deployed measures that echo the kind of mass crimes provoked by the most horrific ethnic cleansing campaigns.[80] The
Stalinist regime continued on this path, reorienting it in two
ways. First, starting in 1937–39, the annihilation of entire populations was primarily focused on communities defined in ethnic terms (Koreans, Tatars, Poles, Finns, Germans, etc.) Second, the practice of mass purges relied on the claim that the
regime's worst enemies had slipped within the party's ranks,
after which their criminal intentions targeting the proletariat
class had become undetectable. Stalin himself designated the
regime's worst adversaries as indiscernible, invisible, and in
possession of a party card in order to better destroy the party.[81]

The appearance of the anti-Semitism at the very core of the
Soviet system, as manifested at the end of the World War II,
incorporated forms and formulas borrowed from the tsarist
tradition and Nazi propaganda alike. The main character of
Vasily Grossman's *Life and Fate*, Viktor Pavlovitch Strum,
comes to this very realization. Strum's alarming discovery of
the anti-Semitism rampant in the USSR in the midst of the
war drives him to reinterpret the social revolution, to which he
had previously adhered, as a process of racialization:

One thing I am certain of: it's terrible to kill someone simply because he's a Jew. They're people like any others—
good, bad, gifted, stupid, solid, cheerful, kind, sensitive,

greedy. . . . Hitler says none of that matters—all that matters is that they're Jewish. And I protest with my whole being. But then we have the same principle: what matters is whether or not you're the son of an aristocrat, the son of a merchant, the son of a kulak; and whether you're good-natured, wicked, gifted, kind, stupid, happy, is neither here nor there. And we're not talking about the merchants, priests and aristocrats themselves—but about their children and grandchildren. Does noble blood run in one's veins like Jewishness? Is one a priest or a merchant by heredity? Nonsense![82]

Disagreements between Soviet history specialists arise from differing opinions on the actual nature of wrong class origins—in other words, the hereditary nature of social positions. They also stem from the distinction between ethnic cleansings deployed as a strategy to eliminate external threats along the empire's borders and Nazi-type exterminations. Yet the confrontation between Leninism-Stalinism and Hitlerism weighs far too heavily on scientific discussion (as on memories). It's easy to understand why comparisons to Nazism determine the very framework of all approaches to the issue of race in the USSR—after all, doesn't *Life and Fate* raise the question as well? If the unit of measurement for racism is the destruction of Europe's Jews, then all other political systems suffer by comparison. In relation to Nazism, any other racial policy can undoubtedly be considered moderate, malleable, and negotiable.

If the historiographical discussion on Soviet racial policies remains captive to the mirror image of Nazism, it is unlikely that the subjects in question will shed light on one another. The sidestep offered by early modern history can provide historians the chance for critical reflection minus the constant pressure imposed by the Hitler-Stalin vise. Broadly speaking, it's clear that the mobilization of racial factors was in direct contradiction with the type of teleological, universalist thinking formulated by Christian doctrine and socialist ideology. In both cases, fixism, which remains a fundamental element of racial thinking, challenged the efficacy of grace and baptism and the revolution's ability to birth an entirely new society. Although racial policies were enacted within Christian societies as well as in Marxist-Leninist systems, racist theories therein remained heteronomous. In both cases, a somewhat external contradiction existed between the belief in universality and the theory of immutability, as in between the hierarchy of conditions in the earthly city and equality in the celestial city. Whereas, if a contradiction was present with the context of Nazism—for example, the concurrent theory of racial immutability and an obsessive fear of racial degeneration—it remained largely internal, meaning internal to racism itself. In this regard, Nazism and Leninism-Stalinism are not equivalent.

The universalism of Christianity and socialism thus share the same antinomy with racial thought. The spiritual and historical mission of the church has been proselytic, prompting since its establishment practices of conversion and missions aimed at transforming those capable of hearing the truth of the Gospels. Nothing could have been stranger to that system than a notion of man that predicated his inability to change. Soviet communism claimed it could give birth to the future of Russia according to historical laws of transformation that would wipe out the past, individuals and communities alike, and start with a clean slate. How could this ideology admit that revolutionary transformation might not have been able to reach many of those individuals or communities? But, if truth be told, all forms of universalism inevitably confront a similar contradiction. Islam, for example, cannot escape this fundamental tension; no more than can the conscience and institutions of the French Republic striving to manage the colonial populations of its empire; or the American ideal of freedom and the status of African Americans and Native Americans.

Is it worth it to, if not compare, at least use the examples of the Soviet system and the Iberian incarnation of the *res publica christiana* during the Renaissance to shed light on their racial policies? Several factors indicate yes. We can take two possible directions. The first focuses on the more or less significant role played by an individual's family origin in evaluating the position he or she merits in society and political institutions. In this regard, both early modern Iberian societies and the contemporary Soviet system produced norms, adopted procedures, and forged ideologies that tended to naturalize social and cultural differences. The second, and undoubtedly more singular, angle concentrates on the role of slavery and forced (or militarized) labor as a tool to transform human material deemed unworthy of Christian communion or socialist citizenship owing to its confinement within a too primitive and animalized humanity.

The parallel suggested here in no way implies the discovery of a little-known legacy: Leninism-Stalinism owes nothing to the history of the Iberian empires, or only in a manner so indirect that the labyrinth of interpositions that separate the two periods rids the search for elements transmitted from the latter to the former of all substance and interest. On the other hand, study of the existence of racial policies using a contradictory institutional and ideological framework, in regards to racial thinking, appears to be a useful endeavor. The identification of racism in systems with universalist aims indicates that political use of racial categories is always marked by strong ambivalence. There are, however, specific exceptions to this rule, such as Nazism, Jim Crow laws in the United States, apartheid in South Africa, and genocides committed for the purposes of ethnic cleansing, starting with the Armenian genocide in the waning Ottoman Empire.

For all that, the fundamental antinomy present in the two historical experiences evoked here should not serve as the expected conclusion of an empirical study. To the contrary, it strikes me as a theoretical point of departure for any investigation on the implementation of racial politics. By accepting, from the start, that racial policies can be deployed in societies whose ideological foundations claim to be universalist and emphasize man's faculty for transformation, we can confidently dissect the contradictory signals found in any empirical materials gathered during the historical investigation of racial policies.[83] From that vantage point, any historiographical criticism that attempts to identify the exceptions, normative inconsistencies, violations, frauds, and imprecisions within racial mechanisms in order to refute the racial character of those same policies appears far from convincing. In their major work on the "anthropology of Nazism," Édouard Conte and Cornelia Essner conclude that the racial politics and ideologies of a supreme racist regime would be characterized by profound contradictions manifested as practical and theoretical inconsistencies:

> The genesis of the Nuremberg laws is instructive. . . . There is no doubt that the statutes' authors were aware they were attempting to fit a square peg in a round hole. Here, as elsewhere, the term of "race" was deliberately used by the regime as an overarching principle that allowed its followers' ideal, and sometimes contradictory, visions of identity to be subsumed under the same "collector term." . . . This was done in order to facilitate the coexistence of two orientations of racial politics that reflected initially heterogeneous premises, i.e., "genetics" and "contagionism."[84]

Likewise, if there is no doubt that racial laws passed in many US states after the Civil War instituted racist systems, the fact remains that the legal and jurisprudential basis for said systems has never been purged of internal inconsistencies. Take, for example, miscegenation laws and subsequent legal decisions, which, as demonstrated by Peggy Pascoe, illustrate the cruel and chaotic nature of these statutes, as well as their moral intransigence and confused application.[85] It goes without saying that the majority of racial policies are flawed on the technical level and unsound or rife with contradictions on the ideological level. But they are not any less based on racial categories. Of course, the mechanisms of domination and segregation evoked earlier are always accompanied by social, religious, cultural, and/or economic considerations that owe nothing to the laws of heredity but that can be squared with them, or with what is believed to be known about them. From this perspective, we cannot rely on the seeming coherence of contemporary racism in order to distinguish it from older forms, which are reputedly less coherent and as a result are categorized within a "pre-" or "proto-" racial era. In both the early modern and contemporary eras, race should have never provided consistence or substance to the structuring of Christian societies or socialist systems, in either practice or theory. Contradiction, then, is our starting point.

CHAPTER THREE

Toward a Nonlinear
History of Race

WHEN THE REJECTION of religious converts, the inferiorization of colonized peoples, and the expulsion of slaves to the
fringes of a shared humanity are viewed collectively, a nonlinear approach unfolds in the sense that it does not lead from
a minimal manifestation of the question of race to the maximum represented by the Jim Crow–Nazism–apartheid trio.
The analytical definitions proposed in the previous chapter
(under "Race: Object or Category?") lend themselves to the
identification of a morphology of modes of racial thought,
as well as to the historical study of sociopolitical and normative practices that implemented programs of racialization of
groups and individuals.

Suppose, for example, that we use "war of the races" as the
common theme of this history. In this case, a certain number
of specific episodes must be studied, beginning with events
during the first English revolution and the crisis of the French
aristocracy in the early eighteenth century, as highlighted
by Hannah Arendt and later by Michel Foucault.[1] Next, it's

essential to address the exclusion of Iberian new Christians and the relegation of mixed-race individuals to lowly positions in the colonies from the very beginning of Europe's overseas presence. Historical research can now propose an amplification of the theme of the war of the races, opening it to a period much earlier than the seventeenth century of the English revolution and opening it to other spaces, starting with the Iberian Peninsula, and the colonies of the Iberian monarchies. In opening the theme thus, the picture of the history of racialization processes is enriched and freed from a linear conception that the West has progressed from a minimum of racism (in early modern times) to a maximum of racism (in contemporary times).

As historians, we may want to free ourselves from two dialectics that have heavily influenced the philosophy of history: the prosopopoeia of the human mind revealed to itself and the primitive accumulation of capital. By doing so, we can approach the study of the expressions of race-based policies from a nonlinear perspective. That said, this approach does not confine our study to the hypothesis of an inflexible discontinuity between the observed phenomena. The point is not to revive the debate on the comparisons and connections between, for example, the two major forms of European anti-Semitism, situated during Iberia's Golden Age and German nationalism. Two positions on this question appear too radical to be maintained. The first, quite popular among a number of Spanish and Latin American historians, consists of rejecting all parallels between persecution of the fifteenth to eighteenth centuries and more recent racist regimes, thereby transforming what is, to them, a commonly held belief into axiom.[2] The second lays out a sort of genealogy that places inquisitors and those who wrote the statues of blood purity in direct relationship, of sorts, with theoreticians of German racial superiority in the 1930s.[3] Neither of these two stances fits perfectly, as is shown by Yosef Yerushalmi in his famous essay, cited above.[4] If we consider the social, religious, and political mobility of families who abandoned Judaism to better (and in vain) find their place alongside, and blend with, Christian families, be it in fifteenth-century Spain or Wilhelmian and Weimar Germany, then the two contexts facilitate understanding of the other. In both cases, the production of a theory of race appears to have been fostered by the success of attempts to assimilate one segment of the Jewish or converted minority into the non-Jewish majority. And in both cases, because their alterity had faded, Jews underwent phenomena of alteration. In order to avoid restraining one's historical imagination, it's essential to allow ourselves the intellectual freedom to detect paroxysmal forms of symbolic or physical violence against human groups under the heading of racial theories across different eras.

A previous work of mine, on the transformation of the topography of barbarism in the sixteenth century, runs along similar lines.[5] In that instance, my objective was to show that points of reference inherited from antiquity, and based on Herodotus's geography of civilization (the center) and barbarism (the periphery), were disrupted by the waves of anxiety provoked by the splendor and power of the Ottoman Empire, the brutality of the conquest of the Americas, and religious civil wars within Europe. The narrative of the general ubiquity of barbarism or the descent into a new iron age is the focus of several major literary works from the end of the century: Montaigne's *Essays*, Shakespeare's tragedies, Cervantes's novels, Las Casas's denunciations, Blaise de Montluc's bloody chronicles, Agrippa Aubigné's tragic epic poem, and Irish plantation owner Edmund Spenser's fiery reprobations, among other testimonials of the passions of the time. For those interested in the turmoil described by these late sixteenth-century masters, there is little doubt that a pinnacle in perception of human debasement had been reached.

The pyres glowing red across Spain in the 1560s and the "open season" against Jews in Portugal during the 1630s marked an early peak in real debasement; the treatment of Andean Indians beginning in 1530 and Portuguese raids into Brazil's hinterlands in search of slaves marked others. And what can we say about the deportation of Africans to the Americas? Even if it is indisputable that the slave trade reached its peak between 1770 and 1820, the dehumanization inflicted by the plantation system did not, for all that, wait for the triangular trade to reach its apex. The actors of all these practices relied on racial thinking to justify the unjustifiable, according to various temporalities and rhythms.

Themes Recurrent in the Historical Study of Racial Policies

In racial reasoning, targeted individuals and populations cannot control traits attributed to them at birth as if they were transitory states that a subject can overcome through willpower. Social mobility, cultural mutual influence, and even social interactions and political concessions—in short, all the variable elements of social processes—are affected by inborn traits and can be, at first glance, absorbed into the black hole of racial categorization. Nazism, in its turn, is an irresistible object of historical reflection on racial categories and fuels the notion that not only do racial policies know their targets, but that a natural hierarchy of human beings frames the correlating political measures and social stratification. If that is the implicit theoretical model, it's easy to understand why so many historians who study ancient societies are reluctant to qualify processes of stigmatization as racial, even when their

physiological or biological foundations are explicit. Many researchers pay close attention to the agency of the victims of
segregation and persecution, studying how people were able to
escape in part or even completely the status that their position
in the racial and social hierarchy assigned to them. Therefore,
these authors prefer to observe the existence of margins of ma-
neuver that, they think, relativized in practice the effectiveness
of the rules of segregation. And, of course, the infinite variety
of individual life experiences composes a social picture made
up of innumerable nuances, in the face of systems of regulation that are both simple and general. If the price to pay for
accepting the descriptor of "racial" is admitting a reduction of
social complexity, both in terms of the multiplicity of discrim-
inating criteria and of victims' capacities to react, then we can
understand some historians' reticence. But, as shown by many
authors, it is possible to identify racial statutes and measures,
both early and recent, without sacrificing the complexity of sociopolitical configurations on which the establishment of hierarchical relations is based. Max Hering Torres's work on blood
purity in Spain, as well as on social stratification in Spanish
America, is a perfect example. The pages that follow, while
far from exhaustive, provide an idea of how that complexity is
taken into account even when the notion of race penetrates the
domain of social analysis.

{⸘⸘⸘W⸘⸘⸘}

The rejection of specific segments of society always occurs to
the benefit of other segments. The advantages gained to the
detriment of segregated groups are not solely material. The
balance of power revealed by segregation also takes the form of
an ideological victory, or, in other words, the triumph of values
held by the beneficiaries of segregation. That is why victims

of stigmatization, as a matter of principle, are attributed values other than those claimed by their persecutors. But material benefits and ideological domination are not the only two drivers of discriminatory measures. If we examine the political uses of racial categories in the early modern era, it is apparent that operations of differentiation like election of "one's betters" and the stigmatization of outcasts all bring natural causality into play (in short: the blue blood of the nobility, according to the French expression,[6] and the blood impurity of individuals of dubious origins, according to the Iberian model). This shared characteristic can sustain a system in which election and stigmatization work together, to a degree, within society. In this case, the act of belonging, for natural or biological reasons, to a group that has been elected incurs a political advantage, not least of all because among the advantages enjoyed by the select few, the power to designate which families deserve to be sidelined is significant. Hence the importance of identifying the possible links between the operations of election and stigmatization, in regards to natural causality, or rather to racial categorization according to the definition maintained throughout this work.[7]

In this sense, stigmatization fits into the hypothesis of the natural fixity of the human condition, believed to be irrefutable by any social (or historical) event. Scientific debate on the origin of man—a single origin (monogenism) versus many (polygenism)—unparalleled since the beginning of the twentieth century, took place within this framework. As discussed in chapter 1, it is clear that the polygenic perspective on the history of humanity appeared particularly suitable to a political project aimed at keeping seemingly distinct populations separated. And by consequence, polygenism was the perfect theory for a fixist ideology and would therefore be the theory the most apt to justify segregation, hierarchization, and slavery, whereas monogenism would better align with universalism and an understanding of evolution. In reality, however, both perspectives have been used to support racial ideologies.[8]

Contradictorily, stigmatization can also result from the idea that accidents of existence can modify a person's essence in a negative way, again as discussed in chapter 1. This was the belief that acquired characteristics or conditions like slavery could be passed through generations and a people could become permanently inferior through history, like the Jews, whose nature was supposedly transformed by incapacity to recognized Jesus's divine nature and his resurrection.[9]

On the other side of the coin, the dialectic of change and permanence makes it possible to understand a political and social process that has played a central role in the history of Western societies: ennobling. In the West, nobility was understood to be a permanent status in lineages, reflecting fixist perspective. In theory, true nobility was regarded as an eternal state, whose origins could not be traced and evidence of which was stated or recorded in an autoregulated social space. Contradictorily, royal ideology claimed to uphold the idea that a certain type of activity was ennobling. The royalty derived a part of its authority from the king's ability to identify and recognize those whose conduct was that of nobles but who had not yet the status of them. Belonging to a good lineage and filling the right role each helped establish the other and were ensured and reinforced by the congenital transmission of virtues and a guarantee of recognition by the royal institution. However, theories about nobility inevitably confront the internal contradiction of accession: when someone is formally granted nobility by order of the king, wasn't he or she already a noble person before being recognized as such? In this case, royal grace can be understood as an agent of transformation and a change of nature—in other words a miracle. But these miracles themselves do not always erase reputations: as long as everyone remembers that someone was made noble, the value of his or her nobility cannot be compared to that of people whose nobility dates back to times immemorial. In the dialectic of perenniality and change, it is the first that wins.

Stigmatization and election therefore rely on systems of causality that the natural sciences attempted—very slowly—to break down. Mutation (or miracle or revolution), the innate fixity of one's condition, and the heritability of acquired traits were all compatible within the political ideologies of the early modern age. These three forms of description of human diversity have become progressively contradictory in modern times. Here, the historian confronts a difficult archeological task. He or she must attempt to work backward to the foundations of the science of natural evolution based on experimentation, established by figures ranging from Jean-Baptiste Lamarck to Charles Darwin to August Weismann, by identifying these scientific scholars in their own time and context, a period that now appears quite distant from our own.

While never entirely symmetrical, the two systems of stigmatization and election nonetheless boast a number of links. For society's stakeholders, operations of sociopolitical reproduction, notably marriage, were crucial to maintaining or improving one's position. In the case of stigmatization, alliances could help create distance from the wrong inherited position; election served to strengthen family honor passed down through generations. In early modern Iberian societies, the procedures to confirm a lineage's noble origins and the procedures to verify that a family did not include persons marked by stigma (Jews, Muslims, heretics, bastards) were identical. The *probanza* (in Castilian), *probança* (in Portuguese), or probationary investigation served these two purposes, regardless of whether a subject sought, for example, to join a military order or to avoid the suspicions of the Inquisition, or lastly, was undertaking the first in order to permanently appease suspicions. Though undoubtedly limited, this model can nonetheless serve as a framework, namely because by projecting the implications of this system, we can imagine that for a commoner living during Iberia's Golden Age, ennoblement was valuable both as an escape from the lower social classes and a way to further protect oneself from the risk of being assigned an identity as a new Christian. If this hypothesis is correct, we would then be dealing with a configuration similar to the ternary system analyzed by Norbert Elias and John Scotson in *The Established and the Outsider*.[10] Their study demonstrates how a well-rooted urban working class would attempt to come closer to the local bourgeoisie, its historic rival, in order to better distinguish itself from migrant working families that settled in poorer neighborhoods, taking advantage of the displacement of certain industries during World War II. Thus, the majority of the lower classes adhered to the social and political values of the dominant sectors of society in order to keep those more disadvantaged than them distant and separate. An analogous system would explain the boundless quest for privilege and honor in Iberian societies, whose actors desired above all to escape any suspicion of dubious origin.

Racial categories in European societies and their colonies during the early modern era are reflective of several major sociopolitical processes. While in no way an exhaustive list, three series of historical phenomena are worth highlighting.

The first, from a chronological perspective, concerns converts' entrance into Christian communion, in particular when political events precipitated collective, or mass, conversions.

The question of identifying Christians descended from converted Jews as individuals differentiated by their genealogy
emerged on the Iberian Peninsula beginning in the fourteenth
century. When Muslim populations were first placed under
the authority of Christian kings, they were not forced to convert. After the fall of Granada, however, and during the reign
of the Catholic Monarchs, all Muslims had to choose between
exile and baptism. Of varying social profiles, Muslims shared
their suspicious status as "new Christians" with former Jews
and were referred to as Moriscos. The opposition between old
Christians and new Christians in Iberian societies corresponds
exactly to the model of the "war of the races" reconstituted and
analyzed by Michel Foucault in his 1977 lecture at the Collège
de France.[11] The refusal to consider new Christians as entirely
integrated in Christian communion could have been qualified
as a "schism" that occupied the center of Spanish life.[12]

The second phenomenon concerns the justifications for en-
slaving Africans. Written texts developed arguments for the
natural inferiority that characterized victims of the slave trade.
Perceptions of blacks were still very diverse in the late Middle
Ages, in other words not necessarily negative. But beginning
with the Renaissance, images and stereotypes coaligned with
increasingly demeaning models as the slave trade and the appearance of free blacks in America became more prominent.
A complete analysis of this evolution would require reestab-
lishing what Christianity in the Mediterranean owes Islam in
terms of stigmatization and the enslavement of blacks.[13]

The third phenomenon relates to the obsessive fear of mixing in the colonies. In general, this fear focused on the risk
of debasement of colonizers on foreign soil under the influence of climates and natural environments.[14] But particular
emphasis was placed on the negative consequences of interbreeding provoked by the birth of children from relations

between colonizers and colonized or from the transformation of colonists' children entrusted to the care of wet nurses from colonized populations. At that time, the partially shameful or barbaric ancestry of mixed-race persons was regarded as a threat to the whole of society.

Early modernist historiography has produced a model of this process within the framework of American societies.[15] However, as demonstrated by Robert Bartlett, intra-European medieval history displays the same kind of configurations.[16] One of the most exemplary cases is undoubtedly the relationship between Anglo-Norman colonizers and the colonized Irish beginning in the thirteenth century, though racial categorization, in the strict sense of the term that I have been using throughout this book, does not play as central a role when a group is judged to be savage, barbarian, and heretical but remains visibly distinct and separate, despite the mobilization of processes of conversion, religious missions, and interbreeding. This could apply to the Moriscos of Spain, the Repúblicas de Indios in the Spanish Empire, and even allied or enemy tribes in the British Empire in America. The fact that racial categories were less applicable in these cases in no way signifies that practices of domination were any gentler.

{~~~~~~~}

In a historical study of the formation of racial categories, the major sociopolitical processes identified above must be examined alongside several of the mental frameworks of imperial and colonial Europe. Three of those frameworks helped to forge political ideologies based on racial differences.

The first is the conception of the individual as part of a lineage and the resulting obsession with genealogy: The fundamental link that connects a person to his or her ancestors does not require that physical evidence be established. Physiognomy can be modified in accordance with one's natural environment (e.g., climate) or social environment (i.e., through finery, clothing, cosmetics); social roles can by all appearances contradict the identity substantiated by genealogy (decline or success); but the seminal chain cannot be erased. This genealogical rationality nourished the fantasy that natural conditions were fixed and omnipresent beneath the surface despite vagaries that could superficially modify an individual's social status or physiognomy.

The second mental framework derives from the use of colors as a metaphorical translation of abstract or moral qualities. Thus, for example, the golden tint, with its capacity to reflect light, expresses the excellence of the virtues and the renown of the people. Conversely, black color, with its ability to absorb light, refers to fear and can mean what is low in society. In the history of race and racism in the West, the battery of negative meanings of the color black predates any empirical reality of physical difference between Europeans and Africans in relation to skin color: for example, night as a time of terror and memory of primordial chaos, and black as the symbol of the devil or of sin. The different processes and periods during which Africans assumed and incarnated these negative meanings are neither simple, nor linear, nor continuous. It is therefore always a very delicate task, albeit a necessary one, to identify the links between the color black as a metaphor for evil and the black man as the incarnation of a condemned humanity.[17]

The third framework incorporates the various versions of an evolutionary understanding of history, which date back to the Renaissance and the Enlightenment and thus owe nothing to Darwinism. These considered the diversity of human societies in terms of gradations that man must or can cross from a state of savagery to one of civility (the latter meaning civilization from the mid-eighteenth century). Fear of a reversibility of the progress made by societies and of the resistance of colonized peoples to adopting the beliefs and mores of their dominators nourished, among the latter group, political ideology on racial differences.

   These three frameworks used to describe human diversity— genealogy, color, and metamorphosis—are the basis of the combinations that formed the backbone of racial ideologies in Europe and its colonies in the modern era and beyond.

Racism as Genealogy and the Making of Invisible Difference

The idea of an intergenerational transmission of social traits is based on an ordinary experience: the physical resemblance of children to their parents. Before the genetic mechanism was described from the 1960s, all kinds of theories since Hippocrates and Galen tried to explain the empirical fact of the reproduction in the child of the physical traits of his or her parents. The notion of transmission must be understood in a positive sense, the inheritance of superior qualities, as much as in a negative sense, the inheritance of infamous qualities. When the question of the formation of racial categories is addressed by the problem of intergenerational transmission, it is impossible to limit the period of deployment of racism to the modern age. Returning to the question of the chronology of racialization, determining the correct chronology is, quite rightly, a point of discord between historians, as has been discussed in previous chapters. As a result, this is an endeavor that can teach us a great deal. Here, it's a question of knowing whether or not it is pertinent to restrict the use of notions of race or racial categories to a relatively recent period. Take, for example, a remark made in passing, in a footnote, by Ann Laura Stoler on the distinction between periods:

Clearly the notion of race in the seventeenth- and eighteenth-century colonies did not bear the same explanatory weight as it does in the nineteenth century. In the former, race is folded into Christian hierarchies of civility, a piece of a larger narrative in which the economics of slavery played a crucial role. By the nineteenth century, race organizes the grammar of difference.[18]

This chronological breakdown employs a conventional distinction between an era during which the question of race emerged in conjunction with other elements and a hyperracial period that coincided with a new wave of colonialism in the nineteenth century. It's remarkable that the author of this proposition does not even envisage the possibility of reaching back to the tail end of the sixteenth century, just before the English and Dutch fleets began their oceanic exploration. Stoler falls victim to the same blind spot as Michel Foucault, who in his 1977 lecture failed to consider the hypothesis that the "war of the races" model could facilitate understanding of European and colonial phenomena prior to the period of the first English revolution.

Must we then consider that discriminatory reasoning in the medieval and early modern eras is too tainted by theological, cultural, and social elements to allow for a more recent conception of alterity determined by natural transmission, and excluding all other markers, to emerge? This argument misses its mark, not because medieval and early modern racism was not entangled in wider social forces, but because racism in the twentieth century, even in its most absolute expressions, took stock of the attitudes, beliefs, and political dispositions associated with offending genetic heritages and believed that these factors exposed others' social incompatibility with the persecuting society. If contemporary racial categories are interspersed with nonnaturalist considerations, then why should we restrict historians to arguing that racial categories unadulterated by any other considerations were established in past political systems, and that those periods did not dispose of racial categories within the arsenal of sociopolitical domination.

David Nirenberg points out the flaw of this reasoning perfectly:

> In modern history, the practice of defining race in a reductionist manner to better eliminate it has succeeded in effectively paralyzing the practices of comparatism and analogy, on which, however, rests all study on the relationships between ancient and contemporary forms of discrimination.[19]

In his recent book on the now famous anti-Semitic writings in Martin Heidegger's "Black Notebooks," Peter Trawny judges that he can distinguish between, on the one hand, racist anti-Semitism, both popular (in the pornographic version of Julius Streicher's *Stürmer*) and pseudoscientific (in Alfred Rosenberg's *The Myth of the Twentieth Century*), and, on the other hand, philosophical anti-Semitism ("anti-Semitism inscribed in the history of being").[20] Insofar as it is "inscribed in the history of being," the perception of Judaism evokes race, albeit in a nonbiological acknowledgment. While not forcing us to take a stance on the case of Heidegger, the distinction made by Trawny challenges the historian. Therefore we won't ask ourselves what the assumption of the existence of a modified philosophical anti-Semitism could mean in a context where popular and pseudoscientific anti-Semitism constituted the backbone of a state-cum-dictatorship, but rather: if there was room for a nonracial form of anti-Semitism during the Third Reich, then what precisely is stopping us from admitting the existence of purely spiritual hostility toward Jews and their converted descendants in sixteenth-century Spain, regardless of statutes on blood purity, the circulation of pamphlets hostile to converts designated as perpetual Jews, and waves of legal executions carried out by the Inquisition? Can we truly retain the hypothesis of an anti-Semitism based only on spiritual distrust, entirely innocent of racial thinking in these political contexts? In the debate between historians on this point, little agreement is forthcoming between those who regard the persecution of Iberian new Christians (Jews and Muslims) as a mix of religious distrust and opportunism and those who interpret these practices as the deployment of a racial policy. To those who dismiss the hypothesis that early modern Spain's anti-Jewish elite may have adhered to biological racism as absurd and anachronistic, one could respond: and what about Martin Heidegger? Did he conceive of Judaism in just these spirituals terms?

Here, we should modify our questions slightly. In order to find a solution to the problem of chronology, it can be very helpful to examine proposals made by historians of the natural sciences. To borrow Maurice Olender's formula in *Razza e destino*, biology acted as a "divine metaphor," providing both scientific legitimacy and a way to simplify the study of the process of racialization:[21] hence the value of drawing lessons from the broad international study of scientific doctrines on heredity, led by Staffan Müller-Wille and Hans-Jörg Rheinberger at the Max Planck Institute for the History of Science in Berlin since the beginning of the 2000s. Upon close inspection of the aims behind this massive project and its initial results gathered in the volume *Heredity Produced*, it is clear that the history of the formation of the concept of heredity cannot, through analogy, be substituted for that of racial policies. The scope of the former is situated halfway between the far too long duration of the legal conception of inheritance and the far too recent history of experimental genetics. In fact, the asymmetry between the centuries-long validity of heredity as a legal concept of patrimonial transmission and its very recent biological and medical significance provides the framework of the analysis. Müller-Wille and Rheinberger's project, like my own, therefore explores a kind of middle ground that encompasses a substantial period of European history. That said, there is no reason to superimpose conclusions on the appearance of the organic conception of heredity on those related to the emergence of racial policies:

> Heredity has become entrenched as a fundamental notion of twentieth-century biology. This creates both the illusion that heredity must have been recognized as such since time immemorial, and the converse view, that there was no concept of heredity to speak of before the advent of genetics. . . . [This book] extends over the period in which heredity, formerly a concept restricted to the realm of law, began to be applied as a metaphor in matters of organic reproduction and successively became a concept of central importance to the life and human sciences. We identify the beginning of this period with the emergence of racial classifications in early sixteenth-century Spain and Portugal, and its end with the appearance of general biological theories of heredity in the second third of the nineteenth century.[22]

Thus the appearance of "racial classifications" in Iberian societies can be dated to the sixteenth century (in reality, one could argue that the fifteenth century also deserves inclusion in this chronology) by the authors, who situate the perfect transposition of patrimonial heritage to organic heredity in the beginning of the nineteenth century. Sarah Eigen Figal comes to the same conclusion in her study on heredity, race, and the birth of the modern. She limits her field of research to German society during the long eighteenth century. As a philosopher, Figal is particularly attentive to legal doctrines on heredity and the legitimacy of children, the natural sciences, and major literary creations in German society during the Enlightenment. Through intensive analysis of one society and one period, she rediscovers a much longer chronology of genealogical thinking, which encompasses all of Europe:

> The societal structure of early-modern Europe was to a great extent organized by laws regulating property and officially recorded identity through consanguineous, and specifically paternal, lines of inheritance. The right to own land, to practice a craft or profession, to study, to marry, to inhabit a particular region or city, even one's status as a freeman or a serf, was legally determined by one's pedigree. In sum, the position of an individual within a genealogical line mapped that person's regulative identity.[23]

Thus, it doesn't appear all that difficult to link the signification of inheritance in civil (meaning patrimonial) law with the physiological meaning of heredity around the system of genealogy. We can no longer posit that techniques to certify an individual's origins were merely a preoccupation among those who feared the impact of a possible loss in status. Rather, those techniques framed and accompanied the intergenerational reproduction of signs of belonging and, by consequence, played a central role in family life at the intersection of civil law and illusions about transmission through blood.[24] In this context, Ariela Gross shows that racist usage of the law in the United States was built not on a sharpened understanding of hematology, or any other branch of medical science, but on a game of legislation and jurisprudence.[25]

Naomi Zack constructs her analysis of the efficacy of the
hierarchy of race in the United States on the basis of the
asymmetry between social inferences drawn from a white
and black genealogy, respectively.[26] Her model is based on
contemporary race relations and shows that the existence of
a black ancestor suffices to tarnish a citizen's racial identity,
to the point of making him or her "black," regardless of actual skin color, whereas the existence of a white ancestor in a
black lineage does not "whiten" the descendants and, in any
case, can certainly not transform them into "white" citizens.
This asymmetrical mechanism to assign color-based identity
has long coexisted with designations to express the degree of interbreeding of individuals (half-blood, quadroon, etc.).[27] But
neither the arithmetic nomenclature of the dilution of blood
nor the asymmetric functioning of racial assignation resulted
from the social sphere's contamination by naturalism or the
experimental sciences. In both cases, we are dealing with arguments of a racial nature independent of any biological theory
based on the concept of heredity. In other words, a genealogical analytical framework, though simultaneous with the development of the sciences of heredity, can be applied without
the slightest contact with said sciences. Once again, the political and racial management of the Jewish question in Iberian
societies in the late Middle Ages can be a useful cross-check.
Indeed, the same asymmetrical mechanism was deployed four
centuries earlier in the confrontation between the genealogies
of new Christians and old Christians. For example, one Jewish
ancestor was enough to Judaize an entire lineage, whereas an
old Christian ancestor could in no way correct the wrong nature of a lineage.

The history of scientific doctrines must always accompany
the study of the political uses of race. However, it is important
to avoid viewing one of the two approaches as the measure

of the other. It is more useful to consider how chronological frameworks and entry points into the subject of race are
connected. If a historian chooses to focus on the domain of
color or physiognomy, then his or her interpretation will tend
to date the appearance of racial categories to the eighteenth
century, even if expressions of opinions on skin color can be
observed during the medieval period. For example, in Bruce
Baum's remarkable study on the ideological construction of
the "Caucasian" category as a racial subdivision, his interpre-
tative framework builds on a color-based line of questioning,
which produces a specific chronology:

> There was no notion of a Caucasian race in the years be-
> tween 1000 to 1684. In fact, the "race" concept itself was
> introduced by European elites only near the end of this
> period, in the seventeenth century, after the rise of the
> Atlantic slave trade and massive enslavement of "black"
> Africans.[28]

This position prompts two objections, the first being the
refusal to reduce the question of racial thought to opposition
between Europeans (whites) and Africans (blacks), the second,
a reminder that African slave markets hit their peak on the
Iberian Peninsula in the second half of the fifteenth century, or
a good two centuries before the Royal African Company even
existed in London. Baum's proposition is based on a legitimate
but debatable historiographical foundation. It outlines three
tenets of European racial thought:

> The development of the modern Western scientific project
> of racially classifying people was shaped by a number of
> epochal events: the consolidation during the late Middle
> Ages of the idea of Europe as a geographically distinguish-
> able region within the larger Eurasian land mass; the rise

in the early modern period of Europeans' assumptions of their innate physical, intellectual, cultural, religious and moral superiority—assumptions that European elites reinforced and refined in relation to European "discoveries" of the indigenous peoples of the Americas, the development of modern "Negro" slavery, and increasing European colonization of the Americas, Africa, and Asia; and the gradual growth and diffusion of a world capitalist economy.[29]

Nothing could be less evident than the emergence of the idea of Europe in the late Middle Ages, except perhaps an awareness of a "Eurasian land mass." The confrontation with Islam, both territorial and deterritorialized, appears to be a much more relevant criterion. But beyond this relatively secondary point, the three elements designated as the building blocks of the European racial conscience—Eurocentrism, colonialism, and capitalism—are in fact also contemporary characteristics, even though Baum formally situates them in the Middle Ages and the Renaissance. Furthermore, without launching into a debate on the possible errors produced by anachronisms, it's clear that the three phenomena defined above anchor racial thinking exclusively to the relationship to geographical and civilizational exteriority. Even as Baum accords great importance to the notion of "racialization," his reasoning does not acknowledge the possibility that racial thought was based on operations of intra-European distinction and segregation—the most debatable point in his study. Baum builds his chronology and geography around an argument drawn from the work of George Fredrickson, according to which slavery during the Renaissance did not solely target blacks and did not rely on a dynamic of racialization of blacks. From this proposition, indisputable on the basis of widely accepted historical sources, Baum draws the conclusion that the link between slavery and race was not yet fully developed, and by consequence the notion of race was not fully formed. He attributes, again not without historical arguments, the formalization of this link to English plantation owners in Virginia and the Caribbean who adopted regulations and laws beginning in the 1660s on the servile and naturally inferior status of Africans in the Americas. But Baum fails to note the circular nature of his line of reasoning: race as a political concept is the result of the slave trade, yet the link between race and the enslavement of blacks belatedly appears in the British colonies, and by consequence the concept of race is itself delayed. The idea that the British colonies might not have been the pivotal point for the history of race doesn't occur to Baum.[30] Rather, he holds that everything that came before in the history of European practices of racialization is a sort of prehistory of the racial issue in the West. This blind spot in his reasoning stems less from an Afro-centrism prompted by the importance of the African American experience in the twentieth century than by a well-established historiographical Anglocentrism. If Baum had integrated the historical depth of the Iberian experience, that is, exclusion of converted Jews and Moriscos and the treatment of persons with mixed blood in the Americas, his chronology would no doubt have been different. In this aspect, he does not follow Fredrickson's lead, though he claims to.

To better measure what is at stake in the debate over chronology, let's look at a second example drawn from a famous essay. In a book published in 1989, Tzvetan Todorov defined "racialism" as an ideology based on five premises: (1) races are a reality; (2) there is a continuity between what is physical and what is moral; (3) the action of the group weighs on the individual; (4) a unique hierarchy of values forms this ethnocentrism; (5) political action must be based on this scientific knowledge. According to Todorov, the ensemble of these traits constitutes "racialist" thinking. From there, he identifies the racist nature of a conflict when two factors are present: the visible difference of a minority within a society and the dominated (or dominant) position of that group. Drawing from the primacy given to the visible nature of otherness, Todorov reflects on the case of hostility toward Jews, which warrants commentary:

> Anti-Semitism is a special problem. On the one hand, "Semites," unlike blacks, possess no strikingly obvious characteristics (hence the Nazis' need to require them to wear the yellow star: how could they have been recognized otherwise?); thus the discrimination is purely cultural (a question of religion, mores, and so on), and cannot be included within classical racism. On the other hand, racists have established the category of the "Semitic race"; they have chosen to be anti-Semites (rather than Judeophobes, for example); and the "Semitic" case is the most serious one in the history of racialism. We are thus obliged to take it into account in our investigation of racial theories.[31]

The above excerpt constitutes a stand-alone paragraph in the introduction to the chapter "Race and Racism" and has not been shortened. It flips conventional thinking on its head by situating the phenomenon of anti-Semitism outside the circle of racist thought, or in a pinch on its periphery. It participates, willingly or not, in a phenomenon highlighted by Les Back and John Solomos in their reader on social theories of race:

> One of the regrettable features of much contemporary theorising about race and racism has been the tendency to leave the question of anti-semitism to one side, treating it almost as a separate issue. This is in spite of the fact that one of the most consistent themes that runs through

racist thinking and the values articulated by racist and fascist movements throughout this century has been anti-semitism.[32]

This schism between scholarship on racism and on anti-Semitism is all the more unfortunate because it appears to overlook the fact that the battle against both scourges was long conducted in a unified and solidary manner.[33] What is the source of the discomfort that inspires Todorov's paragraph? Let's begin by noting the inner tension: according to the first sentence, anti-Semitism is not part of the classical history of racism; however, according to the second sentence, it is one of the most important chapters in the history of "racialism," hence our obligation to take it into account. On the one hand, the sequence of Todorov's arguments attempts to erase the distinction, which can be viewed as both debatable and fragile, between "racism," "racialism," and "racial theories." The author himself suggests this nomenclature, which does little to prevent him from switching one expression for another. On the other hand, the first sentence of the paragraph appears to date clothing markers worn by Jews to the Nazi period alone, with no mention of the existence of similar laws in medieval Christendom between the fourteenth and fifteen centuries (the wearing of circular badges, for example). Finally—and this is the most important point—the first sentence proffers an argument that can be expressed as follows: because Jewish difference is not visible—like that of blacks—then discrimination against Jews is "cultural" and not racial. It is this equivalence between the visibility of alterity and racial explanations that warrants commentary, namely because the argument can very well be completely inverted.

In fact, awareness of the physical alterity of blacks or Africans is attested to by a variety of iconographical supports. The best-known example remains the pictorial convention of depicting Balthazar the wise man as an African, beginning in the fourteenth century. Study of this immense iconographical corpus reveals its vast diversity, from the representation of the dignified African to portraiture that depicts him as lowly and threatening.[34] Awareness of visible alterity thus does not necessarily imply the presence of the five elements that, according to Tzvetan Todorov, are the components of rac(ial)ist thought. Therefore, racism against blacks does not stem from visible evidence of alterity, but from two sociopolitical phenomena that can be identified and dated: first, the confrontation between American plantation owners' desire to see their slaves' children born into servile status and evangelical universalism, the invention of individuals' accidental reduction to slavery, and the growing diffusion of abolitionist arguments at the turn of the seventeenth and eighteenth centuries; second, the surge in freed blacks after emancipation, the real and imagined effects of the Haitian Revolution, the strides made by the abolitionist movement in the United States, and finally, after the Civil War, the immediate and unconditional citizenship granted to slaves freed en masse that prompted theories, rules, and laws to organize political society according to strict parameters of racial segregation. Therefore, the most powerful motor driving racism against blacks would have been the rapprochement of the black condition and shared citizenship in postslavery societies. In other words, racism against blacks in this context was less a discrimination based on differences than a rejection of process to reduce the distance between dominated and dominant groups. Rules aimed at forbidding free people of color from bearing arms or, more simply, to dress in the same fashion as Europeans during the Ancien Régime are equally symptomatic of this phenomenon.

Now, if we apply the same reasoning to the Jewish question, the phenomenon of invisibility appears to follow a parallel trajectory. In fact, both the medieval circular badge and the mark of the yellow star resulted in making something that had become invisible through time and dissimulation visible again, and that a new discriminatory policy hoped to reveal to a community by that point blind to the differences in question. From that point on, the relationship between racial thought and invisibility appears to be stronger. One could even posit that racial reasoning serves above all the necessity to reveal differences that the eye can no longer identify. It is a political response fitting a social phenomenon judged to be threatening. Medieval Jews were marked and forced to live in specific areas, in order to compensate for the impossibility of recognizing them. Converted Jews on the Iberian Peninsula and in the Americas were attributed lineages said to be "tainted," even as it was no longer possible to either mark them or forbid them from settling where they wanted. Here we can see the common element in anti-Jewish racism and antiblack racism. In both cases, racial thought aimed less to highlight a visible alterity than to create a new form of alterity in response to the elimination of these minorities' differences from the sociopolitical order.

Or, to echo Maurice Olender, the singularity of racial thought lies in "the immediate correlation that [it] claims to establish between the visible and the invisible."[35]

In his study on the expulsion of Spanish Jews, Norman Roth responds, in his manner, to the question raised by Yosef Yerushalmi on the possible link between Iberian anti-Judaism and contemporary anti-Semitism. Roth first qualifies the analogy between anti-Semitic racism in the nineteenth and twentieth centuries and hostile attitudes toward Jews in the late Middle Ages as an "anachronism" and suggests that the presence of Jewish communities was not then perceived as the persistence of a race. Roth then immediately asserts that by emphasizing

that Jewish blood was tainted, laws on blood purity "some-
how created a *racial* inferiority." (Note that the author himself
underlined use of the term *racial*.[36]) He concludes that the
term "anti-Semitism" can be used to designate the system of
political discrimination conceived to target converted Jews,
but not to describe religious antipathy toward the synagogue.
His proposed solution to the problematic of two types of anti-
Semitism—the Iberian model during the Renaissance and the
Nazi one—is neither evasive nor paradoxical. Rather, Roth
maintains that it's precisely the elimination of the Jewish difference that nourished the naturalist or genealogical imagination. In other words, racial thought was a response to the
imperative to produce alterity in contexts in which it was no
longer evident.

Anthropologist Juan Aranzadi defines "popular racism"
as a "sylvan ethnocentrism" based on sensory experience. He
places it in opposition to "scientific racism" (a concept I prefer
to avoid, as previously noted), which, unable to rely on sensory
impressions, sublimates them into a fantastical conception of
physical interiority. Thus, the genealogical argument appears
to be the response to the imperceptibility of difference:

> Scientific racism . . . by choosing genetic heritage as a ra-
> cial determinant, becomes completely abstract, theoretical,
> ideal, imperceptible, occult, lodged within the most im-
> penetrable intimacy of the body, the biological factor that
> defines race. Nothing is more ideological, yet completely
> removed from the sensory world.[37]

An example borrowed from our contemporary history—two
Jewish statutes promulgated by the French Vichy regime on
October 3, 1940, and June 2, 1941, respectively[38]—illustrates
the central role of visibility in the implementation of anti-
Semitic policies. A 1942 article by Maurice Duverger, a French

political scientist and professor of public law, published in
Revue de droit public on "the position of civil servants since
the revolution of 1940" reintroduced a very old argument:

> If religious criteria are adopted, the risk is that the majority
> of Jews will fake a seeming conversion and thus manage to
> elude application of the law.[39]

Duverger observed that June 25, 1940, was set as the date
by which to verify Jewish religious affiliation, in other words
before the end of the republican regime:

> This last measure can be explained by the fact that count-
> less Jews converted after the armistice, in an attempt to
> circumvent legislation concerning them: this calculation is
> thwarted by the fact that the law considers that all con-
> versions following June 25, 1940, are not to be taken into
> consideration.[40]

He added:

> The status of Jews results in a distinction between nation-
> als belonging to the Jewish race and nationals belonging to
> the French race. Henceforth the principle of equal access
> to civil service will apply only to the latter. The reason that
> Jews cannot hold civil service positions is the same reason
> that naturalized citizens cannot: to protect the interest of
> the civil services. . . . However, the measures taken in regards
> to Jews are stricter and more intensive than those taken in
> regards to naturalized citizens. This can be explained by the
> fact that Jews have been judged a greater political danger
> than naturalized citizens: the public interest thus necessi-
> tates the adoption of stricter regulations concerning Jews.[41]

There's no need to comment at length about the rationale
shared by Maurice Duverger and the racist American judges

who implemented Jim Crow laws, as well as by the inquisitors of the early modern era who hunted Judaizers disguised
as honest Christians in Iberian societies. After all, we know
that the question of identifying Jews continued until the collapse of the collaborator regime in occupied France. The anti-
Semitic physician George Montandon nourished the Institute
for the Study of Jewish and Ethno-racial Questions with his
wild theories about anthropometric measurements capable
of revealing anyone's Jewish origin. Those measurements fall
within the domain of visibility, albeit on a millimeter scale.
However, evidence of Jewishness, meaning the faculty to be
recognized, is not in fact evident. That reality drove George
Montandon to publish a brochure entitled "How to Recognize and Explain the Jew?" in 1940, which also announced a
forthcoming manuscript under the title "Jewish Ethnicity or
Whorish Ethnicity."[42] The difficulty came from the fact that
everyone already knew what a Jew was supposed to look like
thanks to the presence of graphic and literary caricatures in
Europe since the 1940s. But at the same time, the public of
bons Français, or good French citizens, needed to be equipped
with a manual to help them recognize the people whose appearance they believed they already knew. In the same way, in
1942 police officers and occupying forces imposed the wearing
of yellow stars not only for reasons of targeted persecution, but
also to reveal Jews' imperceptible or invisible belonging to the
same race to everyone else. Consider how Montandon tries to
dialectically overcome this problem:

> We all know the potential results of domesticating animals,
> in terms of the development, diminishment, and modifi-
> cation of various traits, while continually favoring cross-
> breeding between subjects presenting the aforementioned
> traits in the desired sense. But, as has been recognized in

anthropology for several years, an analogous phenomenon occurs, albeit attenuated, among groups of humans who, having long practiced intermarrying, have, so to speak, spontaneously cultivated such and such a trait already well developed among them. In anthropology, we refer to this phenomenon as self-domestication. Particular characteristics of the populations of certain nations can be explained by self-domestication. This process also allows us to understand the emphasis and fixity of certain Jewish traits.[43]

It's tempting to compare this text to Buffon's well-known passage on the degeneration of animals, notably in relation to domestication, which begins with these famous words:

> The state of domesticity largely contributed to color variation among animals, which are in general originally tawny or black; the dog, the steer, the goat, the ewe, the horse have taken on all kinds of coloring; the pig changed from black to white; it appears that the color white, pure and without spots, is in this respect the sign of the final degree of degeneration.[44]

It's doubtful that any racist thinkers, so quick to borrow naturalist material to boost their fanciful theories, would have appreciated this passage.

We can link Montandon's brochure to an event that took place in Paris from September 5, 1941, to January 15, 1942, with his participation: "The Jew and France" exhibition was organized at the Palais Berlitz and modeled after "Der ewige Jude" ("The Eternal Jew"), an exhibition held in the library of the German Museum in Munich in 1937. Our knowledge of the Paris exposition comes from newsreels of the period and a brochure.[45] It has received continuous attention from specialists on the history of the Vichy regime.[46] For our purposes, however, the important point is the contradiction between publicity posters advertising the event and the content of the exhibition. The ads depict caricatures or stereotypes of the Jew as a figure recognizable by the shape of his or her nose, the curve of his or her spine, and the grip of his or her claw-like hands. However, the exhibition panels juxtapose photographs of well-known Jewish figures arranged by profession (politicians, artists, lawyers, industrialists, bankers, etc.). The panels clearly had the pedagogical aim of showing that individuals descended from Jewish families were present in all professions, as if it were a social anomaly and a concerted political project, but also served the didactical function of helping visitors identify the supposedly typical traits of Jewish faces and silhouettes. The critical point is evident: the exhibition's mission was to teach the public how to recognize people said to be identifiable at first glance.

However, as demonstrated in Joseph Losey's film *Mr. Klein*, there are two ways to approach the question of race: first, the practice of anthropometry as depicted by the film's opening scene, or in other words the affirmation of the recognizable, and by consequence visible, character of racial differences; and second, family research of the kind Mr. Klein conducts on his own genealogy, though he never obtains an entirely clear answer, from either an aging parent or archival materials. For analytical purposes, I distinguish between anthropometric evidence and familial research, though it's well known that repressive bureaucracies combined them in order to identify individuals targeted by persecutions.

Racial policies lead to two operations: identifying individuals' specific features in terms of which groups they belong to and then asserting that those traits are transmitted from generation to generation. This kind of analysis has been progressively constructed since the Renaissance, to the point of provoking the creation of charts listing the human races or classification frameworks. Both the physical transmission of cultural traits and the elaboration of hierarchies between groups can be situated within political dynamics. Indeed, that is how two long-term sociopolitical and socioeconomic phenomena give rise to racial ideologies. The first is persecution on the basis of religious, cultural, and social discrimination, as both a government technique and a method to produce a social order. The second is exclusion of populations from a shared humanity prompted by a dominant economic system that demands their enslavement. In both cases, the use of categories is intended to create distinctions within one territory or area, meaning in tangible proximity. The obsessive fear of mixing or crossbreeding provides more than enough evidence of the fact that racial thought is first applied to the perception a society has of itself.

Color and Mixing Bloods: "Métissage" Everywhere, Racial Democracy Nowhere

The Western Christian world transformed itself by crossing oceans. Questions of alterity, which had been an interior, liminal concern, became an imperial and colonial one beginning in the late Middle Ages. Racially based policies that had been established within European kingdoms thus contributed to shaping the colonial system. Even as nothing of the racialized past was forgotten, new social realities were established in terms of how Europeans acted and observed others away from home. Within the historical stratification of phenomena that constitute the political deployment of race, the colonial period was the era when focus shifted to color and métissage. As in previous chapters, the following pages are not meant to offer a narrative of these phenomena, but rather to provide a few keys to understanding how historians can approach such processes.

If the analytical framework proposed here is accurate, what role should we attribute to skin color in the genesis of racial thought? Merely asking this question and, what's more, at this stage of analysis will no doubt surprise the majority of authors who have addressed the topic of race within the cultural, academic, and political context of Anglophone universities, and notably within the United States. As I have observed in previous chapters, it is striking to note that the vast majority of American social science studies that address the question of race establish a kind of equivalence, so evident as to even be tacit, between race and color. In contrast, studies on Iberian blood purity fall within specific fields including research on Jewish history, the history of the Inquisition, the Marranos, or the Moriscos, but not the broad field of race scholarship.

Thus, to borrow a distinction proposed by Claude-Olivier Doron, predominant social science literature on racial categories tackles the question of how alterity of the other is handled, particularly in its perceptible dimension, but not production of alterity within the self (or alteration), whose manifestations are not necessarily perceptible.[47] The equivalence, or even interchangeability, between differences and *visible* differences is reinforced by a vast literature of cognitive and evolutionist psychology that investigates the mind's disposition, in theory, to make phenotypic distinctions and interpret them, again in theory, as innate capabilities/ability.[48] Indeed, experimental studies with cohorts of children are based on the subjects' reactions when confronted with the appearance of a visible difference. As Ian Hacking wryly notes:

Yet one cannot but suspect that they underestimate how quickly very young children catch on to what is wanted of them. One might say, with a whiff of irony, that children have an innate ability to figure out what adults are up to, and hence manipulate the experimenters.[49]

If young children taking this kind of test display an initial disposition to distinguish people according to phenotype, it may also be a manifestation of their ability to reproduce stereotypes seen on television. Whether one believes in the relevance of these studies or is wary of their protocols, it is clear that they approach the subject of race from, dare I say it, a chromatic perspective, which reflects an American obsession but certainly does not encompass the subject of racial categorization.

If social science studies of racial discrimination were established within a framework based on color, the pioneering work of W.E.B. Du Bois and, in particular, the following well-known and prescient passage, was undoubtedly influential:

The problem of the twentieth century is the problem of the color-line,—the relation of the darker to the lighter races of men in Asia and Africa, in America and the islands of the sea. It was a phase of this problem that caused the Civil War; and however much they who marched South and North in 1861 may have fixed on the technical points of union and local autonomy as a shibboleth, all nevertheless knew, as we know, that the question of Negro slavery was the real cause of the conflict. Curious it was, too, how this deeper question ever forced itself to the surface despite effort and disclaimer. No sooner had Northern armies touched Southern soil than this old question, newly guised, sprang from the earth,—What shall be done with Negroes? Peremptory military commands, this way and that, could not answer the query; the Emancipation Proclamation seemed but to broaden and intensify the difficulties; and the War Amendments made the Negro problems of today.[50]

From the moment we approach the history of racism from the color angle, three dimensions risk being undervalued: the dynamics of invisibility, the importance of genealogy, and the chronological depth of racism. As shown by Magali Bessone, these elements don't emerge immediately, meaning that for W.E.B. Du Bois, color was indissociable from both perceptible experience and social and political constructions.[51] This in no way implies minimizing the fundamental importance of perception of skin color and other morphological aspects—to the contrary. In Stephen Cornell and Douglas Hartmann's volume on ethnicity and race, they note that visible difference places the individual, labeled according to his or her apparent physiological difference, in the situation of being unable to entirely get rid of his or her "condition" in life, to borrow a term from Pap N'Diaye.[52] The fact that we cannot not see that a black person is black in a European society, or that a white person is white in an Asian society, is not an unimportant phenomenon. Perceptual processes have a considerable impact on a person's sociopolitical experience, regardless of the extent of his or her capability to conform to dominant sociopolitical and cultural standards, and regardless of the disposition of individuals in a majority group to be disinclined to reduce every individual in a minority group to the same visibly distinct type.

Immediately visible difference, even if it can appear to be a generalized experience, particularly after five centuries of colonization and the massive mobilization of slave labor, is the result of specific situations. The claim that it is the generic mode of racial distinction in Western societies inevitably stumbles over logical and historical obstacles. The greater the observed perceptible differences the less practices of discrimination, repression, or categorization are forced to rely on biological arguments. Again, the historical approach I propose consists of demonstrating that racism based on visible differences is rooted in an earlier history that consists of the racist response to the invisibility of the other, and whose primary investigative tool was genealogical techniques. In other words, at the moment colonial societies were feeling a need to theorize the inferiority of blacks by assigning them a natural and genetically transmittable identity, European societies, notably Iberian ones, had for a long time already understood the efficacy of a genealogical conception of alterity, used to perpetuate the stigma of the unfaithful Jew through traits of natural dispositions transmitted through generations.

This theory is not meant to establish a kind of primacy of anti-Semitism—as self-loathing in the Western world—over negrophobia or contempt for Native Americans—as a rejection of the other or an instrumental discourse used by settlers (even if Étienne Balibar suggests analyzing contemporary forms of racism as an extension of anti-Semitism).[53] Instead, I propose a chronology of the emergence of racial categories, as political resources, that situates the phenomenon of Iberian anti-Semitism in a position of de facto antecedence in relation to discriminatory laws established during the formation of colonial societies. That said, this antecedence is not absolute and therefore does not presuppose any discontinuity between one phenomenon and another. On the contrary, the proposed chronology incorporates, as a fundamental historical element, the fact that social groups that founded colonies in the Americas, thanks to a maximum exploitation of native societies and the importation of millions of Africans, had descended from a political culture whose organizational policies accorded the racial rejection of former Jews converted to Christianity a central position.[54] If this chronology accurately takes into account the processes underway in the modern era, then we must conclude that the stigmatization of religious converts is not analogous with the rejection of visibly different populations—for example, blacks. This order of events suggests, counterintuitively, that reprobation of generally imperceptible religious converts was in fact the breeding ground and incubator for disgust or revulsion based on phenotype.

The issue of alterity expressed through skin color is not any less fundamental. However, historians need to seize the tools necessary to understand this field in all its complexity. On the one hand, it's important to address what appears as a universal revulsion at darker coloring, for instance sub-Saharan African skin. Indexations of paleness of members of a superior class not obligated to work outside, as opposed to a suntan that betrays the opposite condition, can be found in numerous societies, including, for example, in eastern Asia. It is equally important to acknowledge that the idea that black skin denotes a nature fated to servility refers to the biblical curse of Ham, but that this was adopted by European societies after being incorporated and conceptualized by medieval Iberian societies.[55] This problematic beginning necessitates reference to the interaction between Christianity and Islam in the Mediterranean region, which, once again, situates the Iberian Peninsula in a strategic position for understanding the historical process in question. Finally, it is essential to incorporate into the analysis the fact that early modern Europeans did not know how to interpret the color of black skin because melanin had not yet been identified.[56] Cosmetic and congenital explanations, for example, the association of an African mother's desire to give birth to a black infant with the existence of artificial skin-darkening techniques, reduced African blackness to desire and culture, and not nature. In the same way, climatic and environmental explanations persisted despite being refuted by experience. While this complicates the white European view of black skin, it in no way refutes the argument that racial ideologies around skin color descended from earlier racial thinking based on the notion of inherited, not necessarily visible difference.

⟨⋙⟩⚊⟨⋘⟩

In 1950, Lucien Febvre and François Crouzet wrote a book at UNESCO's request, which remained in manuscript form for sixty years until its recent publication by Denis Crouzet and Élisabeth Crouzet-Pavan under the title *We All Are Mixed Bloods*.[57] That editorial choice echoes Lucien Febvre's famous note in the French journal *Annales: Économies, sociétés, civilisations* on the anthropological collapse of the "mystique of blood."[58]

Fear of interbreeding concerned the social sciences as much as it did politicians, warned Ashley Montagu in 1942:

"Race" is a dynamic, not a static, condition; . . . it becomes static and classifiable only when a taxonomically minded anthropologist arbitrarily delimits the process of change at his own time level.[59]

Montagu was reacting not only to the horrors of Nazism, but also to the power of institutional and pseudoscientific racism in the United States. The phantasmagoria over the threat of interbreeding found its most famous champion in Madison Grant, an advocate of American eugenics. Waging open war on Franz Boas, Madison, a lawyer and anthropologist, collected his theories on the decline of the Nordic races confronted with peoples of the South in *The Passing of the Great Race; or, The Racial Basis of European History*.[60] This book destined to reorient immigration quota policies in the United States is haunted by the fear that interbreeding will result in the dilution and disappearance of the virtues of Nordic races ("the great race"). From among Grant's proposals, Nazi racial ideologues adopted the idea that sterilization could be an essential weapon to combat the risks of racial hybridity.[61] In his unpublished autobiography, American eugenicist Leon Whitney recounts that Madison Grant showed him a letter from Adolf Hitler in which the Nazi leader called *The Passing of the Great Race* his "Bible."[62]

The appearance of mixed-race individuals, and even mixed-race populations, accompanied the formation of colonial societies from the very beginning of European overseas expansion. These social processes included two kinds of transformation: the supposed reverse evolution of European subjects in the natural and cultural environment of non-European societies; and the birth of children from relations between European men and African, American, and Asian women.

The first phenomenon refers to so-called ensavagement, from the Portuguese *lançados* on the coast of Guinea to Hans Staden's experience among the Tupinambas to captive Mary Rowlandson in New England.[63] The process of Europeans' transformation under the effect of new environments did not begin with expansion into Africa and America. For one, the endeavor of the conquering Spain is fueled by the rejection of the metamorphosis of populations that had been Christian in the time of the Visigothic kings. Closer to the modern colonial dynamic, the evolution of the "Old English," the first Anglo-Norman settlers of the English Pale in Ireland, into the lords of Anglo-Irish culture haunted plantation owners and shaped the policies they adopted during the Elizabethan era.

The second phenomenon refers to the birth of mixed-race children and its political dimension. The appearance of "mixed-bloods" was destined to play a decisive role in the history of the creation of colonial societies, namely as the object of a massive and strategic ideological investment, in particular in regards to the sociogenesis of Latin American societies

following the period of independence. This more recent investment represents a challenge for historical interpretation
of the mixed-race phenomenon during the colonial era.[64] In
effect, the processes at work during the modern era can be
included within the saga of interbreeding, which would retroactively transform the reality of cross-cultural fertilization
and racial mixing into the fruit of a project to create a new
society. However, one wonders if Iberian colonizers, anchored
to the principles of blood purity, believed that the creation of
a mixed population would be a happy ending to their travels
across the sea.[65] Some scholars have gone so far as to claim
that Iberian Catholic colonization of the Americas was aimed
at creating mixed populations. But, during the Ancien Régime,
were Iberian dispositions any more favorable to legitimate
mixed unions than those of the English Puritans or the Dutch?[66]
Given the history I have presented in this book, it would seem
unlikely, but the question is nonetheless worthy of closer
examination.

This question resurfaced in a significant way on Sunday,
May 12, 1985, during a state visit by Pope John Paul II to the
Netherlands. During a homily delivered in Utrecht, the pope
was subjected to invectives from activists, young and old alike,
far-left prochoice youth and far-right Calvinist fundamental-
ists. Several were even arrested for attempting to throw flam-
mable projectiles at the pope's cortege. Pope John Paul II's
response the following day, during an address to the International Court of Justice in The Hague, could not have been
stronger or more explicit:

> For Christians and for all who believe in a Covenant, that
> is, in an unbreakable bond between God and man and be-
> tween all human beings, no form of discrimination—in law
> or in fact—on the basis of race, origin, color, culture, sex or

religion can ever be acceptable. Hence no system of *apart-heid* or separate development will ever be acceptable as a model for the relations between peoples or races.[67]

The use of the Dutch term "apartheid" was evidently not a fortuitous one, as it created a dynamic link between racially discriminatory legislation then in effect in the Republic of South Africa and the Dutch and Calvinist roots of the Afri-kaner National Party. The pope responded to accusations of moral conservatism by invoking the universality of catholic-ity in comparison to the providentialism of certain Protestant movements expressed as white supremacy, in both the United States and South Africa.

Given the context, the pope's argument undoubtedly hit home. However, in a discussion among historians, its inherent contradictions are easily detected. In a study on how the Cath-olic Church's position on Jews changed in twentieth-century Europe, notably central Europe, John Connelly demonstrates how racist theories popular from 1920 to 1945 were received and adapted by intellectual circles and Catholic institutions, particularly in Germany and Austria.[68] The trajectory of Fa-ther Wilhelm Schmidt is a prime example. (Schmidt was the chair of the Department of Ethnology at the University of Vi-enna and then director of the Department of Eugenics at the famous Kaiser Wilhelm Institute of Anthropology, Human Heredity, and Eugenics in Berlin from 1927 to 1933.) Schmidt, an ecclesiastic and a scientist, defined the nature of Jews in terms of their inability to see the truth of the Gospels without straying from official monogenism:

> This kind of transgression can by itself distort the being of
> a people; yet in the case of the Jewish people, the betrayal
> of its high calling has made this distortion go very deep. In
> punishment this people, as Christ himself predicted, was

driven out of its homeland. Almost two thousand years of distortion and uprooting of its essence has then had a secondary but real effect on its physical race. These racial effects . . . are not neutralized by baptism. For that, Jews will have to work hard on themselves. [Converted Jews] may therefore belong to our number, but not in the same way as our German racial comrades.[69]

The question of contemporary Catholicism's receptiveness to modern racist ideologies, as Connelly suggests, is not limited to central Europe. The author stresses that the Catholic Church in the United States conformed to practices required by Jim Crow laws. He further notes that no black citizens were allowed to enroll at any Catholic universities between 1922 and 1936. Barely half a dozen institutions of higher education out of 162 welcomed black students during the 1930s. Eight nursing schools out of three hundred did the same. Pope Pius XI's injunction to foster the emergence of a "native" clergy had a minimal impact; barely a dozen black priests were ordained during that period.[70] The conduct of American Catholic institutions offers little to support the exaggerated opposition between a universal Catholicism well equipped to resist racist policies and a Protestantism—namely Calvinist—whose theological fatalism is consistent with racial determinism.

Postslavery Latin America is clearly distinguishable from the United States in many ways, and notably by the fact that no Ibero-American national governments adopted racist legislation comparable to Jim Crow laws. Moreover, the results of research on legal provisions and the establishment of jurisprudence on mixed marriages reveal that hostility to said unions was harsher in the United States than in numerous Latin American countries between the eighteenth century and the twentieth century.[71] However, it's important to note that

tolerance for mixed marriages in those countries was linked
to the ideological aim of "whitening" the populations of new
Latin American republics.[72] The massive appeal for the arrival
of populations from Europe in the Latin American countries
had the explicit objective of reducing the visible presence of
the native populations and the descendants of the slaves by
increasing the proportion of white citizens and by promoting
mixed marriages that would make clearer the overall chromatic tone of the population. This is what the Argentine president Sarmiento had called the struggle of civilization against
barbarism. In the long run, the aim was not to create a new
society based on the crossing of European, Amerindian, and
African blood, but to dilute the non-European elements until
their complete erasure. In some countries, such as Argentina,
the call to European migrants is parallel to the genocidal campaigns against the inhabitants of the interior, described as
conquering the "desert," as if these regions were not populated.
The elimination of an African presence from Argentina and
Mexico would later appear to be the result of those political
choices. Later, Gilberto Freyre's meditations and the legend of
racial democracy in Brazil, or José de Vasconcelos's praise of
the "cosmic race" of mixed-blood Mexicans, nourished an existing discourse that, for the most part, can be categorized as
myth.[73] As notes political scientist Melissa Nobles, who conducts research on racial segregation in the United States at
the intersection of the social sciences and law, Latin America
would be wrong to exaggerate the extent of its advantage in
terms of nondiscrimination:

> Latin American societies have tended to pride themselves
> on their multiracialism. Although Brazil was for many de-
> cades the largest slaveholding society in the hemisphere,
> and lacked a mass multiparty democracy until 1945, it was

one of the first Latin American countries to declare itself
a racial democracy. The paradoxes of Brazil are typical: The
ideal of racial democracy flourishes most vigorously when
political democracy has not. The rhetoric of multiracialism
has routinely been deployed by oligarchic and authoritar-
ian regimes.[74]

As a result, it's hard to see why historians should interpret the intermixing of Latin American populations as the
result of a coherent history that stretches back to the early
days of colonization. The idea that Catholic colonization of
the New World, in perpetual rivalry with the United States,
was in principle a program of interbreeding has more to do
with anti-Yankee ideology than with serious observation of the
conditions of mixed-race citizens when they first emerged in
the beginning of the sixteenth century.[75] The fact that marriage between European settlers and native Americans was
not prohibited does not signify in any way that such unions
were considered to be a source of honor for the Europeans
concerned. In the study cited above, Verena Stolcke advances
two arguments, whose juxtaposition demands commentary.
On the one hand, she states that the Catholic Monarchs, and
later Charles V, signed decrees protecting settlers from Native
Americans, who—as *gentiles*—were considered to be pure of
blood, which would allow one to consider that no race-based
policies were institutionalized in the conquered territories
in America. On the other hand, Stolcke notes one page later
that the vast majority of children born from unions between
settlers and Native Americans were not recognized by their fathers and as a result became bastards who were viewed as im-
pure in regards to statutes on purity of blood. If nonrecogni-
tion of these children occurred in the majority of cases, then
we are dealing with a social regularity that should be analyzed

not as solely the random outcome of an aggregation of personal decisions, but as a political rule. The widespread relegation of these children to the inferior status of bastards reflects the political organization of the societies in question. In this case, we can argue that a racial policy was applied to them, beginning with the first generation of mixed-blood children in America.[76]

That is why we can invert the traditional perspective that limits racist social engineering in Latin American countries to widespread national whitening campaigns beginning in the last third of the nineteenth century with the importation of European migrants. From the first days of colonization, the Spanish "Republic" in America was designed to grow as a purely European society, alongside native "Republics." The origin of the whitening of the Americas is as old as the conquest itself.

⟨⟫

Thus, the distinction according to the color of the skin has a history, and this differentiation must be put in perspective with other criteria, sometimes older, leading to discrimination. The obsessional rejection of negritude in many colonial and postcolonial societies is closely linked to the history of slavery, of course. But the fact that stigmatization by color is much more present from the end of the seventeenth century than before does not mean that the racial categories were forged only from that moment. If we confuse race and color, we have some arguments to say that racism is a relatively late political reality in the history of the West. On the other hand, if, as I suggest, the emphasis is placed on the importance attached to genealogy, then it becomes possible to find older manifestations of racial segregation, even persecution. Iberian descendants of

converted Jews and American mestizos suffered from such policies long before the issue of phenotype became the main focus
of race.

Race and Change

Thus the history of race and racism in the West results from the
crossing, or rather from the overlapping in the course of time,
of several processes of managing strangeness, whether caused
by those who denounce otherness, or it is found on the basis
of types of indexes that vary over time. We are dealing with
developments that do not follow in a simple or linear fashion. There remains, nevertheless, a discomfiture that is found
in different epochs and contexts: the relationship between
the fixity of nature (from the perspective of a pre-Darwinian
world) and the mutability of social conditions, which, while
not entirely self-contradictory, is more than merely tense. We
can observe that racial thought does not prevent emancipation (even if it impedes it), and that the freedom granted to
certain slaves does not refute the existence of racial prejudice.
Furthermore, we know that descendants of converts managed
to reintegrate into social groups and institutions that had been
forbidden them, despite the laws in effect. In this case as well,
the indelible character of shame or stigma does not block all
advancement. Yet the paradoxical success of certain individuals does not disrupt or change the prejudices pertaining to
their lineage or social group.

The dialectic of fixity and mutability can be expressed in
yet another way when it comes to political philosophy. As observed by George Fredrickson, the question of the use of racial categories takes on a particular aspect in the "West" owing
to the fact that claims of innate inequality between groups
were being deployed in societies that, from the promise of the

Gospel to the declaration of human rights and socialist optimism, had always maintained the notion of a fundamental, even if solely spiritual, equality between all:

> It is uniquely in the West that we find the dialectical interaction between a premise of equality and an intense prejudice toward certain groups that would seem to be a precondition for the full flowering of racism as an ideology or worldview.[77]

The premise of equality must therefore be understood both as a certitude that could be used to bolster any argument refuting racial thought and as the source of an obsessive fear of the intermingling of social statuses—the principal ingredient of racial thought. The system established by Creole society (referring here to descendants of Spanish Europeans born in the Americas) did not recreate nobiliary distinctions, or at least not in the manner in which they were institutionalized on the Iberian Peninsula.[78] Yet creoles promulgated rules and reproduced behaviors that distinguished them as a whole from colonized populations. In the twentieth century, a modern society that claimed to no longer recognize differences between dominator and dominated within itself believed that a new order would grant it a thousand-year future as a society of masters.

In order for a policy to be based on racial distinction, it must necessarily, though not exclusively, include the attribution of immutability. Hegel explained that the Jews' tragic destiny was their result of their "stiff-necked fanaticism," meaning their stubborn refusal to change.[79] Jews were ascribed the role of "passive witness[es]," to cite Maurice Olender, to better measure the progress of the Christian revolution. In other words, Jews were distinguished less by their complicity in deicide than by a condition that would label them permanently as having lived during the Passion of the Christ. But this condition of suspended time is not enough to foster anti-Semitic or anti-Jewish policies.[80] Rather, the formula that adheres most closely to the findings of research on the political history of Western societies is this: the immutability of Jews throughout history is maintained with even greater force when the mobility of Jews is observed within a society, as occurred in a fifteenth-century Spain shaken by civil wars and marked by great social mobility.

In a similar fashion, the attribution of simian animality to blacks became more flagrant as Africans in the Americas came closer to attaining citizenship during the nineteenth century. Alexis de Tocqueville immediately and correctly observed that abolition had prompted an intensification of racial prejudice:

> In that part of the Union where Negroes are no longer slaves, have they drawn nearer to the whites? Any inhabitant of the United States will have noticed just the opposite. Racial prejudice seems to me stronger in those states which have abolished slavery than in those where slavery still exists and nowhere is it as intolerant as in those states where slavery has never been known. It is true that in the North of the Union the law permits Negroes and whites to contract legal marriages but public opinion regards any white man united with a Negress as disgraced and it would be difficult to quote an example of such an event. In almost all the states where slavery has been abolished, voting rights have been granted to the Negro but, if he comes forward to vote, he risks his life.[81]

Tocqueville's narrative and analysis provide an early glimpse of the analogous dialectic between a legal environment and the political and social distance it subsequently creates. Numerous studies have shown to what extent racist discourse was radicalized between 1830 and 1861, a period characterized by the social impact of abolition in northern states and ideological pressure both aimed at combating continuing slave practices in the South and keen to conquer the West. After the Civil War, a fully postslavery society embarked on Reconstruction. It's worth noting the "postslavery" qualifier, which, beyond serving as a chronological marker, designates a society torn apart by its attempts to integrate populations that had been servile the day before into a collective citizenry.[82] An excellent study conducted by Jean Hébrard and Rebecca Scott that traces the descendants of Rosalie, a slave of the "Poulard nation," reveals how mechanisms of categorization and segregation were transformed, without losing any of their power, before and after emancipation.[83]

In her research on the United States from the end of the nineteenth century to the first six decades of the twentieth century, Peggy Pascoe assesses the long history of miscegenation laws. In fact, she determines that these measures were the longest lasting in all American history. It is therefore possible to compare their force before and after the most fundamental social transformation in that history, in other words the complete abolition of slavery:

> Miscegenation laws, in force from the 1660s through the 1960s, were among the longest lasting of American racial restrictions. They both reflected and produced significant shifts in American racial thinking. Although the first miscegenation laws had been passed in the colonial period, it was not until after the demise of slavery that they began to function as the ultimate sanction of the American system of white supremacy. They burgeoned along with the rise of segregation and the early-twentieth-century devotion to "white purity." At one time or another, 41 American colonies and states enacted them; they blanketed western as well as southern states.[84]

Miscegenation laws appear to be an effective barometer to evaluate the intensity of racial prejudice during the transformation of a society whose members are divided by status to one whose members enjoy the same political rights, at least in theory.

Léon Poliakov developed a theory similar to Tocqueville's that explains the generalized racialization of Jewish populations in Europe as the very consequence of their legal emancipation:

> As long as the Jews actually lived under a special legal régime, they were regarded, in good theological doctrine, as possessing all the attributes of human nature, and the curse hanging over then as being only an expiation, from the point of view of Christian anthropology. It was when they were emancipated and able to mix freely in bourgeois high society that the curse became, under the terms of the new so-called scientific anthropology, a biological difference or inferiority.[85]

Thus, the concept of race, whether it relies on a theological or naturalist line of reasoning, remains entirely and exclusively political, insofar that it aims to regulate the distribution of social position or status. In this sense, its efficacy cannot be correlated uniquely to intellectual advances within the natural sciences in Western culture. No one expresses this fundamental notion better than Michel Leiris:

> The more capable the so-called inferior races prove themselves of attaining emancipation, the more emphatic grows the assertion of racial dogma, stiffened by the coloured races' acquisition of a minimum of political rights or by their emergence as competitors. . . . The source of race prejudice must be sought elsewhere than in the

pseudo-scientific ideas which are less its cause than its expression and . . . are of merely secondary importance as a
means of justifying and commending prejudices.[86]

In *The Languages of Paradise*, Maurice Olender demonstrates that determination of racial identity can be based on
the structure of languages spoken by populations rather than
on physical elements. In this sense, the chronology of the formation of racial categories as political resources cannot be
intrinsically linked to that of advances in experimental biology, as illustrated in stark fashion by the history of the Nazi
regime. If the extermination of six million European Jews was
a sinister technological and administrative success, it also represented the complete failure of the scientific construction of
the identification of Jews. From the preparations behind the
Nuremberg Laws to the last wartime rulings, the scientists of
the Third Reich were never able to provide a biological definition of a Jew. And yet, it can't be said that Germany lacked
well-established and advanced scientific facilities. Whether
it's apocryphal or authentic, the quip attributed to Hermann
Göring, which echoed a remark by Vienna's infamous anti-
Semitic mayor Karl Lueger—"I decide who is a Jew and who
is an Aryan"—shows that political determination superseded
any scientific knowledge. Ultimately, the political operation to
limit the plasticity of human societies, and that of the men
and women within them, in order to politically assign them a
rigid identity prevailed. The process of racialization consists of
transferring the immutability of divine truths, the laws of nature, and the laws of man to the identities attributed to various
peoples, hence its demiurgical character and foundation built
on politics, authority, and the mysticism of sovereignty.

Race and Sameness

RETURNING TO THE THEMES addressed at the beginning of this book, it would be a mistake to postulate that scientific research, notably genetics, harbors the perverse usages extracted by the sorcerer's apprentice, so to speak. The desire for segregation and annihilation in no way necessitated a scientific hypothesis in order to set the most catastrophic outcomes in motion. To conclude, it's useful to once again contemplate Franz Boas's words, notably his insistence that the critical element to understanding the history of human societies consists of not conflating time periods that have little in common. The cleavage cannot be based solely on the opposition between nature and culture. On the one hand, anthropometric research that focused in its time on the development of individuals revealed that dietary improvements sufficed to modify the physiognomy of a population in barely one generation. On the other hand, historical study can identify social and cultural phenomena over a much longer duration. But this perpetuation of the collective when mobilizing a singular history echoes the kind of fiction analyzed by Vincent Descombes. Drawing from the *Port-Royal Logic*, Descombes examines how the identity of modern Romans was retroactively attributed to those living during imperial times:

> For the logicians of Port-Royal, it goes without saying that if they speak of the Romans as a single and same moral person, endowed with a diachronic identity, it is purely fictional or a convention of language. It is only because we imagine Rome as an immaterial body that we can recount the city's history as the history of a single people, an immortal person who can remain alive for centuries thanks to successive generations of Romans.[1]

Franz Boas notes and takes into the greatest consideration the way the sociocultural character of groups and populations is passed down over long periods of time. But he also recognizes the illusory and strictly fictional dimension of contemporary practices of retrospective self-identification with ancestors of a faraway past. Hence, the feeling of historical stability produced by fictional mechanisms of identification with one's ancestors is no less subject to criticism than a claim of identity based on hereditary-type data:

> If we could show how people of exactly the same biological composition react in different types of environment, much might be gained. It seems to me that the data of history create a strong presumption in favor of material changes of mental behavior among peoples of the same genetic composition. The free and easy English of Elizabethan times contrast forcibly with the prudish Mid-Victorian; the Norse Viking and the modern Norwegian do not impress us as the same; the stern Roman republican and his dissolute descendant of imperial times present striking contrasts.[2]

His roles as a practitioner and an advocate of statistical anthropometry in no way hindered Boas from criticizing racist inferences. By focusing his critical attention on such inferences, Boas avoids the facile division of the social science approach into a legitimate line of reflection—the study of societies—and an illegitimate one—the study of hereditary transmission. And by doing so, he turns his back on Anténor Firmin's radical stance:

> Nature mocks the anthropologists and confounds them at the very moment they take those sophisticated measurements, which are at bottom mere puerile games, entertainment rather than serious research.[3]

On the contrary, Boas tackled the complete range of physical anthropology, social anthropology, and ethnolinguistics to better disassemble the elements that, within this grouping of modes of understanding mankind, had been combined in an uncritical manner or, among racists, a malevolent one. His point of departure in a compendium published in 1940 directly addressed the fact that men and women have natural bodies and that they differ in this respect from individual to individual and from group to group. Boas energetically formulates the notion that it was futile to deny the link between a person's body and his or her psyche. His position was therefore not constructivist before its time but simply reflected well-reasoned monism:

> There is no doubt in my mind that there is a very definite association between the biological make-up of the individual and the physiological and psychological functioning of his body. The claim that only social and other environmental conditions determine the reactions of the individual disregards the most elementary observations, like differences in heart beat, basal metabolism or gland development; and mental differences in their relation to extreme anatomical

disturbances of the nervous system. There are organic reasons why individuals differ in their mental behavior.[4]

This position, which reflects the stage of scientific knowledge in the fields of medicine and clinical psychology at the time, can be viewed as the ideal perspective from which to condemn racist thinking. Franz Boas showed that, regardless of general opinion within the natural sciences in the early twentieth century, racist thought was entirely founded on the inferences it established between heteronomous registers:

> There exists an enormous amount of literature dealing with mental characteristics of races. The blond North-Europeans, South Italians, Jews, Negroes, Indians, Chinese have been described as though their mental characteristics were biologically determined. It is true, each population has a certain character that is expressed in its behavior, so that there is a geographical distribution of types of behavior. At the same time we have a geographical distribution of anatomical types, and as a result we find that a selected population can be described as having a certain anatomical type and a certain kind of behavior. This, however, does not justify us in claiming that the anatomical type determines behavior. A great error is committed when we allow ourselves to draw this inference.[5]

Therefore, we must conclude that racial thought, in principle, does not depend on the stage of development of the life sciences (an observation also noted by Michel Leiris in the passage cited earlier). Within the ideological development of racism, the contemporary sciences were mobilized as decorative elements for operations that can be categorized entirely as political propaganda. The only question worth asking, at each stage of the investigation, is whether an incorrect causality has been established. A faithful Spinozist, Franz Boas emphasizes:

> Every people in a certain geographical position has a characteristic bodily form combined with a characteristic mental behavior. This, however, does not prove that both are causally related, unless it can be proved by biological and psychological methods that bodily form determines mental character.[6]

Anthropological study therefore does not consist of purging any biologizing contamination, which would be equivalent to denying mankind's place in the animal kingdom. Rather, it consists of producing an epistemology capable of identifying experimental protocols or statistical data that facilitate understanding of the phenomena of differentiation between men and the investigative mindsets that should not be mobilized:

> It will be seen that that part of human history which manifests itself in the phenomena that are the subject of physical anthropology is by no means identical with that part of history which manifests itself in the phenomena of ethnology and of language. Therefore we must not expect that classification obtained by means of these three methods will be in any way identical. Neither is it proof of the incorrectness of the physical method if the limits of its types overlap the limits of linguistic groups. The three branches of anthropology must proceed each according to its own method.[7]

In the history of discrimination, the naturalistic argument prevails especially where the difference is tenuous. We find it with the case of the Judeo-Converses, among those who considered the conversion of the Jews of Spain to have been a lie. The same is true of those who judged, like Jefferson, that African Americans freed from their condition of slavery could not join a common citizenship. The argument of Jewish blood becomes indispensable when the synagogue no longer exists and the descendants of its worshipers no longer signal themselves. The argument of black blood is imperative when there is nothing that may stop the inclusion of former slaves and their descendants in the political body of the nation. Ultimately, racism uses nature, without metaphor, to slow down in the short to medium term the processes of social mobility whose long-term effects are dreaded. If the privileged instrument is the control of generation, then the call to nature is not symbolic but real. These policies are social engineering. But the arguments drawn from nature are not purely facades. By injecting the natural into the social game, what is sought is a glaciation—or at least a slowdown—of transformation (that is, of history). It is precisely because all racial policies aim at interrupting the course of history that the reflection of historians is an indispensable response.

ACKNOWLEDGMENTS

RACE IS ABOUT POLITICS: LESSONS FROM HISTORY is the result of a decision made with Silvia Sebastiani to temporarily extricate myself from our joint written study on the history of the formation of racial categories in the modern Western era. I am indebted to Silvia not only for my having learned a great deal during this intellectual apprenticeship, but also for my having been momentarily liberated during our shared endeavor. This work is, from start to finish, the fruit of our partnership. Even if it is convention, more or less respected, not to pay tribute to the director of the collection in which one's book appears, it is impossible for me not to highlight the role played by Maurice Olender in my decision to write this book. I do this all the more willingly given that I owe an even greater intellectual debt to the author of *The Languages of Paradise* and *Race and Erudition* than I do to the editor of La Librairie du XXIe siècle collection published by Editions du Seuil.

Of course, the research driving this book includes proposals by historians and other researchers, in accordance with the mission of the School for Advanced Studies in the Social Sciences (or EHESS, its French acronym). Indeed, this endeavor was carried out on both sides of the Atlantic: in Paris, where the majority of the following pages were discussed at length by Catarina Madeira Santos, Cécile Vidal, Natalia Muchnik, Claudia Damasceno Fonseca, Juliette Cadiot, Anne Lafont, Anna Joukovskaia, Gérard Lenclud, Éric Michaud, Sophie Nordmann, Lilia Schwarcz, Roquinaldo Ferreira, Sydney Chalhoub, Ariela Gross, Max Hering Torres, and Giuseppe Marcocci; in Nantes, with Antonio Almeida Mendes and Clément

Thibaud; in Lisbon, with António Manuel Hespanha, Pedro Cardim, Ângela Barreto Xavier, Mafalda Soares da Cunha, and Nuno Monteiro; and at the University of Michigan, with Rebecca Scott, Martha Jones, and Jean Hébrard, to whom this work is dedicated.

In Paris, Lisbon, Seville, Ann Arbor, Rio, Buenos Aires, and Tokyo, various elements of this study were presented to students pursuing their master's degrees or doctorates: their responses provided invaluable support and insight.

This is the final project I conducted under the auspices of the Portuguese Center of Global History (CHAM) in Lisbon, as part of a Foundation for Science and Technology program. I continued my work at the TEPSIS Laboratory of Excellence and the Laboratories of the Americas (UMR 8168) at the School for Advanced Studies in the Social Sciences.

NOTES

Epigraphs

1. Fyodor Dostoevsky, *The Adolescent*, trans. Richard Pevear and Larissa Volokhonsky, New York, Vintage Classics, 2004, p. 142.
2. William Shakespeare, *Anthony and Cleopatra*, *The Oxford Shakespeare*, Oxford, Oxford University Press, 1994, 214.

Introduction: The Current Moment

1. Ania Loomba, "Race and the Possibilities of Comparative Critique," *New Literary History*, 40, 2009, pp. 501–22.
2. Gérard Lenclud, *L'universalisme ou le pari de la raison: Anthropologie, histoire, psychologie*, Paris, EHESS-Seuil-Gallimard, "Hautes études," 2013.
3. François Azouvi, *Le Mythe du grand silence: Auschwitz, les Français, la mémoire*, Paris, Fayard, 2012.
4. Alain Peyrefitte, *C'était de Gaulle*, vol. 1, Paris, de Fallois/Fayard, 1994, p. 52.
5. Magali Bessone, *Sans distinction de race? Une analyse critique du concept de race et de ses effets pratiques*, Paris, Vrin, 2013.
6. Albert Jacquard, "À la recherche d'un contenu pour le mot 'race': La réponse du généticien," in Maurice Olender, ed., *Pour Léon Poliakov: Le racisme mythes et sciences*, Brussels, Editions Complexe, 1981, pp. 31–40.
7. Catherine Bliss, *Race Decoded: The Genomic Fight for Social Justice*, Stanford, CA, Stanford University Press, 2012; Katharina Schramm, David Skinner, and Richard Rottenburg, eds., *Identity Politics and the New Genetics*, New York: Bergahn Books, 2012.
8. François Héran, "France/États-Unis: Deux visions de la statistique des origines et des minorités ethniques," *Santé, Société et Solidarité*, no. 1, 2005, pp. 167–89; François Héran, *Avec l'immigration: Mesurer, débattre, agir*, Paris, La Découverte, 2017.
9. *Trajectoires et origines: Enquête sur la diversité des populations en France*, Cris Beauchemin, Christelle Hamel, and Patrick Simon, dirs., Paris, Institut national d'études démographiques, 2016.
10. Commission nationale consultative des droits de l'Homme, "Report on the Prevention of Racism, Anti-Semitism, and Xenophobia 2015," http://www .cncdh.fr/sites/default/files/les_essentiels_-_report_racism_2015_anglais.pdf.

Chapter 1. A Challenge for the Humanities
and Social Sciences

1. Christophe Cusset and Gérard Salamon, *A la rencontre de l'étranger: L'image de l'Autre chez les Anciens*, Paris, Les Belles Lettres, 2008; Miriam Eliav-Feldon, Benjamin H. Isaac, and Joseph Ziegler, eds., *The Origins of Racism in the West*, Cambridge, Cambridge University Press, 2009.

2. François Hartog, *The Mirror of Herodotus: The Representation of the Other in the Writing of History*, Berkeley, University of California Press, 1988.

3. Niall McKeown, "Seeing Things: Examining the Body of the Slave in Greek Medicine," *Slavery and Abolition*, 23 (2), 2002, pp. 29–40.

4. Marshall Sahlins, *The Use and Abuse of Biology: An Anthropological Critique of Sociobiology*, Ann Arbor, University of Michigan Press, 1976.

5. Charles de Miramon, "Noble Dogs, Noble Blood: The Invention of the Concept of Race in the Late Middle Ages," in Miriam Eliav-Feldon, Benjamin H. Isaac, and Joseph Ziegler, eds., *The Origins of Racism in the West*, Cambridge, Cambridge University Press 2009, p. 209.

6. David Biale, *Blood and Belief: The Circulation of a Symbol between Jews and Christians*, Berkeley, University of California Press, 2007, p. 139; Jean-Paul Lallemand-Stempak, "'Cequi circule entre nous': Don du sang et transfusion aux États-Unis (XIX°–XX°)," in Johanne Charbonneau and Annamaria Fantauzzi, eds., *Les enjeux du don du sang dans le monde*, Paris, Presses de l'EHESP, 2012, pp. 37–56.

7. Nancy Farriss, *Maya Society under Colonial Rule: The Collective Enterprise of Survival*, Princeton, NJ, Princeton University Press, 1984, p. 101.

8. Jean-Paul Demoule, *Mais où sont passés les Indo-Européens? Mythe d'origine de l'Occident*, Paris, Seuil, 2014.

9. Éric Michaud, *Les invasions barbares: Une généalogie de l'histoire de l'art*, Paris, Gallimard, 2015.

10. *Le Monde*, March 11, 2012, http://www.lemonde.fr/election-presiden tielle-2012/article/2012/03/11/hollande-propose-de-supprimer-le-mot-race -dans-la-constitution_1656110_1471069.html.

11. Slate.fr, March 14, 2012, http://www.slate.fr/france/51397/race-consti tution-sarkozy-hollande.

12. Chantal Millon-Delsol, "Pertinence de l'énonciation du mot race dans la Constitution," *Mots/Les langages du politique*, 33, 1992, pp. 257–60, p. 260 cited here.

13. Étienne Balibar, "Le mot race n'est pas 'de trop' dans la Constitution française," *Mots/Les langages du politique*, 33, 1992, pp. 241–56, p. 249 cited here. Emphasis in the original.

14. Ashley Montagu, "The Concept of Race," *American Anthropologist*, n.s., 64–65 (1), 1962, pp. 919–28.

15. Dominique Schnapper, *Qu'est-ce que l'intégration?*, Paris, Gallimard, 2007; Alain Blum, "Resistance to Identity Categorization in France," in David I. Kertzer

and Dominique Arel, eds., *Census and Identity: The Politics of Race, Ethnicity, and Language in National Censuses*, Cambridge, Cambridge University Press, 2001, pp. 121–47; Alain Blum, Alain Desrosières, Catherine Gousseff, and Jacques Magaud, eds., "Compter l'autre," *Histoire & Mesure*, 13 (1/2), 1998 (monograph).

16. Didier Fassin, "Nommer, interpréter: Le sens commun de la question raciale," in Didier Fassin and Éric Fassin, eds., *De la question sociale à la question raciale: Représenter la société française*, Paris, La Découverte, 2006, p. 20.

17. Timothy Lockley, "Race and Slavery," in Robert L. Paquettte and Mark Smith, eds., *Oxford Handbook of Slavery in the Americas*, Oxford, Oxford University Press, 2010, pp. 336–56.

18. Winthrop D. Jordan, *White over Black: American Attitudes toward the Negro, 1550–1812*, Chapel Hill, University of North Carolina Press, 1968.

19. Eric Williams, *Capitalism and Slavery*, Chapel Hill, University of North Carolina Press, 1944; Barbara Jeanne Fields, "Slavery, Race and Ideology in the United States of America," *New Left Review*, 181, 1990, pp. 95–118.

20. Giuliano Gliozzi, *Adamo e il nuovo mondo: La nascita dell'antropologia come ideologia coloniale; Dalle genealogie bibliche alle teorie razziali (1500–1700)*, Florence, La Nuova Italia, 1977.

21. Georges Balandier, "La situation coloniale: Approche théorique," *Cahiers Internationaux de Sociologie*, 51, 1951, pp. 44–79.

22. Rees R. Davies, *Domination and Conquest: The Experience of Ireland, Scotland and Wales 1100–1300*, Cambridge, Cambridge University Press, 1990; Nicholas Canny, *Making Ireland British, 1580–1650*, Oxford, Oxford University Press, 2001.

23. Frantz Fanon, *Peau noire, masques blancs* (1952), in *Œuvres*, Paris, La Découverte, 2012; Albert Memmi, *Portrait du colonisé, précédé du portrait du colonisateur*, Paris, Buchet-Chastel, 1957.

24. Rolena Adorno, *Guaman Poma: Writing and Resistance in Colonial Peru*, Austin, University of Texas Press, 2000; Alfredo Alberdi Vallejo, *El mundo al revés: Guamán Poma anticolonialista*, Berlin, Wissenschaftlicher Verlag, 2010.

25. Silvia Sebastiani, *The Scottish Enlightenment: Race, Gender, and the Limits of Progress*, New York, Palgrave Macmillan, 2013.

26. Lisbet Koerner, *Linnaeus: Nature and Nation*, Cambridge, MA, Harvard University Press, 1999; Thierry Hoquet, *Buffon: Histoire naturelle et philosophie*, Paris, Honoré Champion, 2005.

27. Peggy Pascoe, *What Comes Naturally: Miscegenation Law and the Making of Race in America*, Oxford, Oxford University Press, 2010.

28. Lilia Moritz Schwarcz, *Spectacle of Races: Scientists, Institutions and Racial Theories in Brazil at the End of the 19th Century*, New York, Farrar, Strauss, and Giroux, 1999.

29. Denise Kimber Buell, *Why This New Race: Ethnic Reasoning in Early Christianity*, New York, Columbia University Press, 2005.

30. Bernard Vincent, "Les Morisques grenadins: Une frontière intérieure?" *Castrum*, 4, 1992, pp. 109–26; Isabelle Poutrin, *Convertir les musulmans: Espagne,*

1491–1609, Paris, Presses universitaires de France, 2012; Max S. Hering Torres, "Limpieza de sangre en España: Un modelo de interpretación," in Nikolaus Böttcher, Bernd Hausberger, and Max S. Hering Torres, eds., *El peso de la sangre: Limpios, mestizos y nobles en el mundo hispánico*, Mexico, El Colegio de México, 2011, pp. 29–62.

31. Maurice Kriegel, "Un trait de psychologie sociale dans les pays méditerranéens du bas Moyen Âge: Les juifs comme intouchables," *Annales E.S.C.*, 1976, pp. 326–30; *Les Juifs à la fin du Moyen Âge dans l'Europe méditerranéenne*, Paris, Hachette Littérature, 1979.

32. David Nirenberg, "The Case of Spain and Its Jews," in Margaret R. Greer, Walter D. Mignolo, and Maureen Quilligan, eds., *Rereading the Black Legend: The Discourses of Religious and Racial Difference in the Renaissance Empires*, Chicago, University of Chicago Press, 2007, pp. 71–87.

33. Bernard Vincent, "¿Cuál era el aspecto físico de los Moriscos?," in *Andalucía en la Edad Moderna: Economía y sociedad*, Granada, Diputación Provincial de Granada, 1985, pp. 303–13.

34. Claude-Olivier Doron, *L'homme altéré: Races et dégénérescence (XVIIe-XIXe siècles)*, Seyssel, Champ Vallon, 2016.

35. Benjamin Braude, "Cham et Noé: Race, esclavage et exégèse entre islam, judaïsme et christianisme," *Annales: Histoire, Sciences Sociales*, 2002 (1), pp. 93–125.

36. David H. Aaron, "Early Rabbinic Exegesis on Noah's Son Ham and the So-Called 'Hamitic Myth,'" *Journal of the American Academy of Religion*, 63 (4), 1995, pp. 721–59.

37. George M. Fredrikson, *The Black Image in the White Mind: The Debate on Afro-American Character and Destiny, 1817–1914*, Hanover, NH, Wesleyan University Press, 1971, pp. 58–64, 87–88; Andrew S. Curran, *The Anatomy of Blackness: Science and Slavery in an Age of Enlightenment*, Baltimore, Johns Hopkins University Press, 2011.

38. Emmanuelle Saada, *Les enfants de la colonie: Les métis de l'Empire français entre sujétion et citoyenneté*, Paris, La Découverte, 2007; Silvia Falconieri and Florence Renucci, "L'Autre et la littérature juridique: Juifs et indigènes dans les manuels de droit (XIXe-XXe siècles)," in Anne-Sophie Chambost, ed., *Des traités aux manuels de droit: Une histoire de la littérature juridique comme forme du discours universitaire*, Paris, Lextenso, 2014, pp. 253–74.

39. Richard J. Herrnstein and Charles Murray, *The Bell Curve: Intelligence and Class Structure in American Life*, New York, Free Press, 1994; Arthur R. Jensen, "How Much Can We Boost IQ and Scholastic Achievement?," *Harvard Educational Review*, 39 (1), 1969, pp. 1–123.

40. Nicholas Wade, *A Troublesome Inheritance: Genes, Race, and Human History*, New York, Penguin, 2014.

41. Ibid., p. 48.

42. Ashley Montagu, *Man's Most Dangerous Myth: The Fallacy of Race*, New York, Columbia University Press, 1942, p. 14.

43. Wade, *Troublesome Inheritance*, p. 218.

44. Marshall Sahlins, *Critique de la sociobiologie: Aspects anthropologiques*, Paris, Gallimard, 1980.

45. François Jacob, "Biologie et racisme," *Le Genre humain*, 1, 1981, pp. 66–69; Charles Frankel, "Les enjeux de la sociobiologie," *Le Genre humain*, 1, 1981, pp. 83–93.

46. Marshall Sahlins, "The National Academy of Sciences: Goodbye to All That," *Anthropology Today*, 29, 2013, pp. 1–2.

47. Ullica Segerstrale, *Defenders of the Truth: The Battle for Science in the Sociobiology Debate and Beyond*, Oxford, Oxford University Press, 2000.

48. Jean-Loup Amselle, *L'Ethnicisation de la France*, Paris, Lignes, 2011; Hugues Lagrange, *Le Déni des cultures*, Paris, Seuil, 2010; Michel Kokoreff, "Quartiers et différences culturelles," *La Vie des idées*, January 11, 2011, http://www.laviedesidees.fr/Quartiers-et-differences.html.

49. iGENEA, http://www.igenea.com/en/jews.

50. Genetic Literacy Project, http://www.geneticliteracyproject.org/mission/.

51. Jon Entine, *Taboo: Why Black Athletes Dominate Sports and Why We're Afraid to Talk about It*, New York, Public Affairs, 2000; Jon Entine, *Abraham's Children: Race, Identity, and the DNA of the Chosen People*, New York, Hachette, 2007.

52. Nicolas Martin-Breteau, "'Un laboratoire parfait'? Sport, race et génétique: Le discours sur la différence athlétique aux États-Unis," *Sciences sociales et sport*, 3, 2010, pp. 7–43; Nicolas Martin-Breteau, "Sport, race et politique: Taboo et la réception du discours sur les aptitudes athlétiques des races aux États-Unis," *Le Mouvement social*, 242, 2013, pp. 131–47.

53. Sarah Abel, "À la recherche des identités transatlantiques: Des boucles conceptuelles au croisement de la société, de l'histoire et de la génétique," statement presented to the Laboratoire mondes américains (EHESS), November 20, 2014. Publication forthcoming in the online journal *Nuevos Mundos*.

54. Jacquard, "À la recherche d'un contenu pour le mot 'race': La réponse du généticien," pp. 31–40.

55. Paul Gilroy, *Against Race: Imagining Political Culture beyond the Color Line*, Cambridge, MA, Harvard University Press, p. 52.

56. Gregory Cochran, Jason Hardy, and Henry Harpending, "Natural History of Ashkenazi Intelligence," *Journal of Biosocial Science*, 38 (5), 2006, pp. 659–93; also available at https://www.researchgate.net/publication/6919477_Natural_history_of_Ashkenazi_intelligence.

57. Ibid., 692–93.

58. Ibid., p. 8 of the pdf.

59. Charles Murray, "Jewish Genius," *Commentary*, January 4, 2007, http://www.commentarymagazine.com/article/jewish-genius/.

60. *Economist*, June 2, 2005, http://www.economist.com/node/4032638; *New York Times*, March 12, 2006, http://www.nytimes.com/2006/03/12/weekinreview/the-twists-and-turns-of-history-and-of-dna.html.

61. R. Brian Ferguson, "How Jews Became Smart: Anti-'Natural History of Ashkenazi Intelligence,'" http://www.ncas.rutgers.edu/sites/fasn/files/How%20 Jews%20Became%20Smart%20(2008).pdf.

62. Ibid., p. 32.

63. Ibid., p. 36.

64. Harry Ostrer, *Legacy: A Genetic History of the Jewish People*, Oxford, Oxford University Press, 2012.

65. Noah J. Efron, *A Chosen Calling: Jews in Science in the Twentieth Century*, Baltimore, Johns Hopkins University Press, 2014.

66. Jacques Ruffié, "Sociobiologie et génétique," *Le Monde*, July 11–12, 1979; article from *Encyclopaedia Universalis*, https://universalis.aria.ehess.fr/encyclo pedie/sociobiologie/.

67. Jacques Ruffié, "Anthropologie physique et 'races humaines': Leçon inaugurale au Collège de France," *Social Science Information*, 1973, 12 (7), pp. 7–25, p. 25 cited here.

68. Chris Stringer, *Lone Survivors: How We Came to Be the Only Humans on Earth*, London, Times Books, 2012.

69. Yvan Pandelé, "Un traumatisme transmis de père en fils," *Pour la science*, June 2014, p. 6.

70. Magali Bessone and Daniel Sabbagh, "Les discriminations raciales: Un objet philosophique," in Magali Bessone and Daniel Sabbagh, eds., *Race, racisme, discriminations: Anthologie de textes fondamentaux*, Paris, Hermann, 2015, pp. 5–44.

71. Jean-Louis Sagot-Duvauroux, *On ne naît pas noir, on le devient*, Paris Albin Michel, 2004; Pierre Ndoumaï, *On ne naît pas noir, on le devient: Les métamorphoses d'une idéologie raciste et esclavagiste*, Paris, L'Harmattan, 2007.

72. Dany Laferrière, *Comment faire l'amour avec un nègre sans se fatiguer*, Montréal, VLB Éditeur, 1985, p. 153.

73. Education against Racism Foundation, http://www.thuram.org/site/en /the-foundation/goals/.

74. Forza Nuova, http://www.italiachiamaitalia.it/articoli/detalles/15275 /ForzaONuova%20O%20ministroOKyengeOsiOdimetta%20OitalianiOsiOna sce%20OnonOsiOdiventaE.html.

75. Simone de Beauvoir, *The Second Sex*, trans. Constance Borde and Sheila Malovany-Chevallier, New York, Vintage Books, 2011, p. 283.

76. Ibid., p. 12.

77. Charles Ralph Boxer, *Race Relations in the Portuguese Colonial Empire: 1415–1825*, Oxford, Clarendon, 1963; Charles Ralph Boxer, *Mary and Misogyny: Women in Iberian Expansion Overseas, 1415–1815; Some Facts, Fancies and Personalities*, London, Duckworth, 1975.

78. Colette Guillaumin, *L'Idéologie raciste* (1972), Paris, Gallimard, "Folio-Essais," 2002, pp. 225–42; Londa Schiebinger, *Nature's Body: Gender in the Making of Modern Science*, Boston, Beacon, 1994; Elsa Dorlin, *La Matrice de*

la race: Généalogie sexuelle et coloniale de la nation française, Paris, La Découverte, 2006.

79. Margaret A. Simons, "Beauvoir and the Problem of Racism," in Julie K. Ward and Tommy L. Lott, eds., *Philosophers on Race: Critical Essays*, London, Blackwell, 2002, pp. 260–84.

80. Nigel Gibson, "Losing Sight of the Real: Recasting Merleau-Ponty in Fanon's Critique of Mannoni," in Robert Bernasconi and Sybol Cook, eds., *Race and Racism in Continental Philosophy*, Bloomington, Indiana University Press, 2003, pp. 129–50, p. 135 cited here.

81. Tertullian, *Apologeticum*, XVIII, 4.

82. Erasmus, *De pueris statim ac liberaliter instituendis*, Lyon, S. Gryphium, 1541, p. 15.

83. Benedict de Spinoza, *Political Treatise*, trans. A. H. Gosset, London, G. Bell and Son, 1883.

84. Awad Ibrahim, "One Is Not Born Black: Becoming and the Phenomenon(ology) of Race," *Philosophical Studies in Education*, 35 (1), 2004, pp. 77–87.

85. Ibid., p. 79.

86. Verena Stolcke, "Los mestizos no nacen, se hacen," in Verena Stolcke and Alexandre Coello, eds., *Identidades ambivalentes en América Latina (siglos XVI–XXI)*, Barcelona, Ediciones Bellaterra, pp. 19–58.

87. Margarita Chaves and Marta Zambrano, "From Blanqueamiento to Reindigenización: Paradoxes of Mestizaje and Multiculturalism in Contemporary Colombia," *Revista Europea de Estudios Latinoamericanos y del Caribe*, 80, 2006, pp. 5–23.

88. Véronique Boyer, "Qu'est le *quilombo* aujourd'hui devenu? De la catégorie coloniale au concept anthropologique," *Journal de la société des américanistes*, 96 (2), 2010, pp. 229–51; Véronique Boyer, "L'anthropologie des quilombos et la constitution de 'nouveaux sujets politiques' De l'ethnie à la race et de l'autodéfinition au phénotype," *Civilisations*, 59 (2), 2011, pp. 157–78.

89. Peter Kolchin, "Whiteness Studies I," *Journal de la société des américanistes*, 95, 2009, pp. 117–43; Peter Kolchin, "Whiteness Studies II," *Journal de la société des américanistes*, 95, 2009, pp. 144–63.

90. Ezra Tawill, *The Making of Racial Sentiment: Slavery and the Birth of the Frontier Romance*, Cambridge, Cambridge University Press, 2006, pp. 92–128.

91. Neusa Santos Souza, *Tornar-se negro, ou, As vicissitudes da identidade do negro brasileiro em ascensão social*, Rio de Janeiro, Graal, 1983, p. 77.

92. Sigmund Freud, *The Uncanny*, trans. David McLintock, London, Penguin, 2003, pp. 161–62.

93. Lydia Flem, *Le Racisme*, Paris, MA Éditions, 1985, p. 117; J.-B. Pontalis, "Une tête qui ne revient pas" (interview with Albert Jacquard), in *La Société face au racisme, Le Genre humain*, no. 11, 1984, p. 17.

Chapter 2. Historiographical Debate

1. Juan F. Perea, "The Black/White Binary Paradigm of Race," in Richard Delgado and Jean Stefancic, eds., *Critical Race Theory: The Cutting Edge*, Philadelphia, Temple University Press, 2000, pp. 344–53. Emphasis in the original.

2. Michael James, "Race," *The Stanford Encyclopedia of Philosophy*, winter 2012 edition, Edward N. Zalta, ed., http://plato.stanford.edu/archives/win2012/entries/race.

3. Christian Grataloup, *L'invention des continents: Comment l'Europe a découpé le monde*, Paris, Larousse, 2009; Jean-François Staszak, "Qu'est-ce que l'exotisme?" *Le Globe*, 148, 2008, pp. 7–30.

4. Claude-Olivier Doron and Jean-Paul Lallemand-Stempak, "Un nouveau paradigme de la race?," *La Vie des idées*, March 31, 2014, http://www.laviedesidees.fr/Un-nouveau-paradigme-de-la-race.html.

5. Étienne Balibar, "Y a-t-il un néo-racisme?," in Étienne Balibar and Immanuel Wallerstein, *Race, nation, classe: Les identités ambiguës*, Paris, La Découverte, 1990, p. 33.

6. Lilia Moritz Schwarcz, *O espetáculo das raças: Cientistas, instituições e pensamento racial no Brasil; 1870–1930*, São Paulo, Companhia das Letras, 1993.

7. Maurice Olender, *Race and Erudition*, trans. Jane Marie Todd, Cambridge, MA, Harvard University Press, 2009.

8. Peter Wade, *Race, Nature and Culture: An Anthropological Perspective*, London, Pluto, 2002, p. 37.

9. Claude Lévi-Strauss and Didier Éribon, *Conversations with Lévi-Strauss*, trans. Paula Wissing, Chicago, University of Chicago Press, 1991, p. 150.

10. Miriam Eliav-Feldon, Benjamin H. Isaac, and Joseph Ziegler, eds., *The Origins of Racism in the West*, Cambridge, Cambridge University Press, 2009.

11. Jean Starobinski, "Le mot civilisation," *Le remède dans le mal: Critique de l'artifice à l'âge des Lumières*, Paris, Gallimard, 1989, pp. 11–59; Émile Benveniste, "Civilisation: Contribution à l'histoire d'un mot," *Problèmes de linguistique générale I* (1966), Paris, Gallimard, 1991, pp. 336–45.

12. George M. Fredrickson, *Racism: A Short History*, Princeton, NJ, Princeton University Press, 2002.

13. Ibid., p. 167.

14. Ivan Hannaford, *Race: History of an Idea in the Western Culture*, Baltimore, Johns Hopkins University Press, 1996.

15. Henry Méchoulan, *Le sang de l'autre ou l'honneur de Dieu: Indiens, juifs et morisques au Siècle d'or*, Paris, Fayard, 1979.

16. Adriano Prosperi, *Il seme dell'intolleranza: Ebrei, eretici, selvaggi; Granada 1492*, Rome, Laterza, 2011.

17. Ibid., p. 68.

18. Ibid., p. 109.

19. Maria Luiza Tucci Carneiro, *Preconceito racial em Portugal e Brasil colônia: Os cristãos-novos e o mito da pureza de sangue* (1983), São Paulo, Perspectiva, 2005, p. 47.

20. Nathan Wachtel, *La Foi du souvenir: Labyrinthes marranes*, Paris, Seuil, 2001; Nathan Wachtel, *La Logique des bûchers*, Paris, Seuil, 2009; Nathan Wachtel, *Mémoires marranes*, Paris, Seuil, 2011.

21. Nikolaus Böttcher, Bernd Hausberger, and Max S. Hering Torres, eds., *El peso de la sangre: Limpios, mestizos y nobles en el mundo hispánico*, Mexico D.F., El Colegio de México, Centro de Estudios Históricos, 2011.

22. Michael Omi and Howard Winant, "Racial Formations," in Michael Omi and Howard Winant, eds., *Racial Formation in the United States*, New York, Routledge, 1994, pp. 3–13.

23. Maaike van der Lugt and Charles de Miramon, eds., *L'Hérédité entre Moyen Âge et Époque moderne: Perspectives historiques*, Florence, Sismel, "Micrologus," 27, 2008.

24. Ignacy Sachs, "L'image du Noir dans l'art européen," *Annales: Économies, sociétés, civilisations*, 1969, pp. 883–93. Refer to the archives that resulted from efforts by the W.E.B. Du Bois Institute for African and African American Research of Harvard University, http://www.imageoftheblack.com.

25. Antonella Romano, "Observer, vénérer, servir: Une polémique jésuite autour du Tribunal des mathématiques de Pékin," *Annales: Histoire, sciences sociales*, 59, 2004, pp. 729–56.

26. Francisco Bethencourt, *Racisms: From the Crusades to the Twentieth Century*, Princeton, NJ, Princeton University Press, 2013, pp. 60–61.

27. James Sweet, "The Iberian Roots of American Racist Thought," *William and Mary Quarterly*, ser. 3, 54 (1), 1997, pp. 143–66.

28. Eric Voegelin, *Race and State*, vol. 2 of *The Collected Works of Eric Voegelin*, trans. Ruth Hein, Baton Rouge, Louisiana State University Press, 1997, p. 181.

29. James Q. Whitman, *Hitler's American Model: The United States and the Making of Nazi Race Law*, Princeton, NJ, Princeton University Press, 2017.

30. Yosef Hayim Yerushalmi, *Assimilation and Racial Antisemitism: The Iberian and the German Models*, New York, Leo Baeck Memorial Lecture 26, 1982.

31. Ania Loomba, "Race and the Possibilities of Comparative Critique," *New Literary History*, 40, 2009, pp. 501–22.

32. Frederick Cooper and Ann Laura Stoler, eds., *Tensions of Empire: Colonial Cultures in a Bourgeois World*, Berkeley, University of California Press, 1997.

33. Natalia Muchnik, *De paroles et de gestes: Constructions marranes en terre d'Inquisition*, Paris, Éditions de l'EHESS, 2014.

34. Jean-Frédéric Schaub, "Survivre aux asymétries," in Antoine Lilti, Sabina Loriga, Jean-Frédéric Schaub, and Silvia Sebastiani, eds., *L'expérience historiographique: Autour de Jacques Revel*, Paris, Editions de l'EHESS, 2016, pp. 165–79.

35. Robert Bartlett, "Medieval and Modern Concepts of Race and Ethnicity," *Journal of Medieval and Early Modern Studies*, 31 (1), 2001, pp. 39–56.

36. Erving Goffman, *Stigma: Notes on the Managements of Spoiled Identity*, New York, Simon and Schuster, 1963, p. 128.

37. Laura de Mello e Souza, *O Diabo e a Terra de Santa Cruz: Feitiçaria e religiosidade popular no Brasil colonial*, São Paulo, Companhia das Letras, 1986.

38. Adriano Prosperi, "'*Otras Indias*': Missionari della Controriforma tra contadini e selvaggi," in *America e Apocalisse e altri saggi*, Pisa, Istituti Editoriali Poligrafici Internazionali, 1999, pp. 65–87.

39. António Manuel Hespanha, *Imbecillitas: As bem-aventuranças da inferiodade nas sociedades de Antigo Regime*, São Paulo, Annablume Editora, 2010.

40. Giuliano Gliozzi, *Adamo e il nuovo mondo: La nascita dell'antropologia come ideologia coloniale; Dalle genealogie bibliche alle teorie razziali (1500–1700)*, Florence, La Nuova Italia, 1977.

41. Jennifer L. Morgan, "'Some Could Suckle over Their Shoulder': Male Travelers, Female Bodies, and the Gendering of Racial Ideology, 1500–1770," *William and Mary Quarterly*, ser. 3, 54, 1997, pp. 167–92.

42. Barbara Jeanne Fields, "Slavery, Race and Ideology in the United States of America," *New Left Review*, 181, 1990, p. 99 and p. 112. Thank you to Martha Jones for introducing me to this masterly article during our time teaching together at the University of Michigan.

43. Cécile Vidal, "Francité et situation coloniale: Nation, empire et race en Louisiane (1699–1769)," *Annales: Histoire, sciences sociales*, 2009 (5), pp. 1019–50.

44. Ania Loomba, *Shakespeare, Race, and Colonialism*, Oxford, Oxford University Press, 2002, p. 38.

45. Max Hering Torres, "'Limpieza de Sangre': ¿Racismo en la edad moderna?," *Tiempos Modernos*, 9, 2003 (4), pp. 1–16.

46. Charlotte de Castelnau, *Les Ouvriers d'une vigne stérile: Les jésuites et la conversion des Indiens au Brésil 1580–1620*, Paris, Centre culturel Calouste Gulbenkian—CNCDP, 2000.

47. Michèle Duchet, *Anthropologie et histoire au siècle des Lumières* (1971), afterword by Claude Blanckaert, Paris, Albin Michel, 1995.

48. Gianna Pomata, "Menstruating Men: Similarity and Difference of the Sexes in Early Modern Medicine," in Valeria Finucci and Kevin Brownlee, eds., *Generation and Degeneration: Tropes of Reproduction in Literature and History from Antiquity to Early Modern Europe*, Durham, NC, Duke University Press, 2001, pp. 109–52; Pierre Savy, "'Les juifs ont une queue': sur un thème mineur de la construction de l'altérité juive," *Revue des études juives*, 166, 2007, pp. 175–208.

49. Silvia Sebastiani, *The Scottish Enlightenment: Race, Gender, and the Limits of Progress*, New York, Palgrave Macmillan, 2013, pp. 133–62.

50. Jurgis Baltrušaitis, *Le Moyen Âge fantastique* (1955), Paris, Flammarion, "Champs Arts," 1981; John Block Friedman, *The Monstrous Races in Medieval Art and Thought* (1981), Syracuse, NY, Syracuse University Press, 2000; Vitorino

Magalhães Godinho, *Le Devisement du monde: De la pluralité des espaces à l'espace global de l´humanité (XVe–XVIe siècle)*, Lisbon, Institut Camões, 2000.

51. Silvia Sebastiani, "L'orangoutang, l'esclave et l'humain: une querelle des corps en régime colonial," *L'Atelier du Centre de recherches historiques*, July 2013, http://acrh.revues.org/5265; DOI: 10.4000/acrh.5265; Wulf D. Hund, Charles W. Mills, and Silvia Sebastiani, eds., *Simianization: Apes, Gender, Class, and Race*, Reihe: Racism Analysis—Series B: Yearbooks Bd. 6, Berlin, Lit Verlag, 2015.

52. David Bindman, *Ape to Apollo: Aesthetics and the Idea of Race in the 18th Century*, Ithaca, NY, Cornell University Press, 2002; Anne Lafont, "Histoire de l'art et représentation des Noirs: La double occurrence," *Lumières*, 10, *L'Invention et la représentation des races au XVIIIe siècle*, Isabelle Baudino, ed., 2010, pp. 115–32; Eric Michaud, *Les invasions barbares*, p. 65–112.

53. Pierre Serna, "Droits d'humanité, droits d'animalité à la fin du XVIIIe siècle, ou la matrice du "racisme social" en controverse," *Dix-Huitième Siècle*, 42, 2010, pp. 247–63.

54. Joshua Goode, *Impurity of Blood: Defining Race in Spain, 1870–1930*, Baton Rouge, Louisiana State University Press, 2009, pp. 1–34.

55. Salvador Cayuela Sánchez, "Biopolítica, nazismo, franquismo: Una aproximación comparativa," *Éndoxa: Series Filosóficas*, 28, 2011, pp. 257–86.

56. Joan Ramon Resina, "From Crowd Psychology to Racial Hygiene: The Medicalization of Reaction and the New Spain," in Jeffrey Thompson, ed., *Crowds*, Palo Alto, CA, Stanford University Press, 2006, pp. 225–38.

57. Antonio Vallejo Nágera, *Eugenesia de la Hispanidad y regeneración de la raza*, Editorial Española, S. A. Burgos, 1937, pp. 114–15.

58. Miriam C. Meijer, *Race and Aesthetics in the Anthropology of Petrus Camper (1722–1789)*, Amsterdam, Rodopi, 1999; Claude Blanckaert, "Les vicissitudes de l'angle facial et les débuts de la craniométrie (1765–1875)," *Revue de synthèse*, 108, 1987, pp. 417–53.

59. Nágera, *Eugenesia*, p. 108.

60. Antonio Vallejo Nágera, "Maran-atha," *Divagaciones intrascendentes*, Valladolid, Talleres Tipográficos Cuesta, 1938, pp. 95–98.

61. Ibid.

62. Article by Falangist journalist Eugenio Montes in a May 1933 edition of the *Phalange* journal, cited by Gonzalo Alvarez Chillida, *El Antisemitismo en España: La imagen del judío, 1812–2002*, Madrid, Marcial Pons, 2002, p. 378.

63. Bessone, *Sans distinction de race?*, pp. 1–24.

64. Ronald L. Taylor, "On Race and Society," *Race and Society*, 1, 1998, p. 1.

65. Michel Serres, "Faute," *Libération*, November 19, 2009, http://www.liberation.fr/societe/2009/11/19/faute_594497.

66. Frederick Cooper and Rogers Brubaker, "Identity," in Frederick Cooper, *Colonialism in Question: Theory, Knowledge, History*, Berkeley, University of California Press, 2005, pp. 59–90.

67. Bessone, *Sans distinction de race?*, pp. 151–84.

68. Graham Richards, "Race," in *Racism and Psychology: Towards a Reflexive History*, London, Routledge, 1997, pp. 8–9.

69. Stéphane van Damme, "Un Ancien régime des sciences et des saviors," in *Histoire des sciences et des savoirs*, Dominique Pestre, dir., vol. 1, *De La Renaissance aux Lumières*, Stéphane Van Damme, ed., Paris, Éditions du Seuil, 2015, pp. 19–40.

70. Van der Lugt and de Miramon, *L'hérédité*.

71. Franz Boas, *Race, Language and Culture*, New York, Macmillan, 1940, p. 193.

72. Ian Hacking, "Why Race Still Matters," "On Race," *Daedalus*, 134 (1), 2005, pp. 102–16, p. 104 cited here.

73. Several of the articles cited below were featured in *Slavic Review*, 61 (1), 2002.

74. Terry Martin, "The Origins of Soviet Ethnic Cleansing," *Journal of Modern History*, 70 (4), 1998, pp. 813–61; Nicolas Werth, *La Terreur et le désarroi: Staline et son système*, Paris, Perrin, Tempus, 2007, pp. 222–64.

75. Loren R. Graham, "Science and Values: The Eugenics Movement in Germany and Russia in the 1920s," *American Historical Review*, 82, 1977, pp. 1133–64; Francine Hirsch, "Race without the Practice of Racial Politics," *Slavic Review*, 61 (1), 2002, pp. 30–43.

76. Mark B. Adams, "Eugenics in Russia," 1900–1940," in Mark B. Adams, ed., *The Wellborn Science: Eugenics in Germany, France, Brazil, and Russia*, Oxford, Oxford University Press, 1990, pp. 153–216.

77. Alexandre Sumpf, *De Lénine à Gagarine: Une histoire sociale de l'Union soviétique*, Paris, Gallimard, "Folio Histoire," 2013, p. 49.

78. Peter Holquist, "'Conduct merciless mass terror': Decossackization on the Don, 1919," *Cahiers du monde russe*, 38 (1–2), 1997, pp. 127–62.

79. Michel Heller, *Le Monde concentrationnaire et la Littérature soviétique*, Lausanne, L'Âge d'homme, 1974, p. 112; Mikhail Morukov, "The White Sea–Baltic Canal," in Paul Gregory and Valery Lazarev, eds., *The Economics of Forced Labor: The Soviet Gulag*, Stanford, CA, Hoover Institution Press, 2003, pp. 151–62.

80. Nicolas Werth, *L'Ivrogne et la marchande de fleurs: Autopsie d'un meurtre de masse, 1937–1938*, Paris, Seuil, "Points Histoire," 2011, p. 48.

81. Joseph Stalin, *Works*, vol. 4, *1934–1940*, London, Red Star, 1978, p. 245 and p. 260.

82. Vasily Grossman, *Life and Fate*, trans. Robert Chandler, New York, New York Review of Books, 1985, p. 578.

83. Rebecca Earle, *The Body of the Conquistador: Food, Race and the Colonial Experience in Spanish America, 1492–1700*, Cambridge, Cambridge University Press, 2012, in particular chap. 6, "Mutable Bodies in Spain and the Indies," pp. 187–211.

84. Édouard Conte and Cornelia Essner, *La Quête de la race: une anthropologie du nazisme*, Paris, Hachette, 1995, p. 352.

85. Peggy Pascoe, *What Comes Naturally: Miscegenation Law and the Making of Race in America*, Oxford, Oxford University Press, 2010.

Chapter 3. Toward a Nonlinear History of Race

1. Hannah Arendt, "Race-Thinking before Racism," *Review of Politics*, 6 (1), 1944, pp. 36–73; Michel Foucault, *Il faut défendre la société*, Paris, Gallimard-EHESS-Seuil, "Hautes Études," 1997.

2. Antonio Domínguez Ortiz, *Los Judeoconversos en la España moderna*, Madrid, Mapfre, 1992.

3. Christiane Stallaert, *Ni una gota de sangre impura: La España inquisitorial y la Alemania nazi cara a cara*, Barcelona, Galaxia Gutenberg, "Círculo de Lectores," 2006; Adolfo Kuznitzky, *De la inquisición española a Franco y el Holocausto*, Córdoba (Ar.), Ediciones del Corredor Austral, 2012.

4. Yerushalmi, *Assimilation and Racial Antisemitism*, p. 93.

5. Jean-Frédéric Schaub, " 'Nous, les barbares': Expansion européenne et découverte de la fragilité intérieure," in Patrick Boucheron, ed., *Histoire du monde au XVe siècle*, Paris, Fayard, 2009, pp. 813–29.

6. André Devyver, *Le Sang épuré: les préjugés de race chez les gentilshommes français de l'Ancien Régime, 1560–1720*, Brussels, Éditions de l'université, 1973; Arlette Jouanna, *L'Idée de race en France au XVIe siècle et au début du XVIIe*, Montpellier, 1981; Guillaume Aubert, " 'The Blood of France': Race and Purity of Blood in the French Atlantic World," *William and Mary Quarterly*, ser. 3, 61 (3), 2004, pp. 439–78.

7. José Antonio Guillén Berrendero, "La identificación de la honra en la semántica de los contrarios: noble vs judío en Juan Benito Guardiola y su *Tratado de nobleza* de 1591," *Cadernos de estudos sefarditas*, 10–11, 2010, pp. 389–421.

8. Sebastiani, *Scottish Enlightenment*.

9. Denise Kimber Buell, *Why This New Race: Ethnic Reasoning in Early Christianity*, New York, Columbia University Press, 2005.

10. Norbert Elias and John L. Scotson, *The Established and the Outsiders*, London, Sage, 1994.

11. The lecture from 1977 appears in Foucault, *Il faut défendre la société*.

12. Rica Amran, "Sobre algunos puntos de vista de cristianos nuevos y viejos en el siglo XV: El cisma castellano de 1449," in Maria Filomena Lopes de Barros and José Hinojosa Montalvo, eds., *Minorias étnico-religiosas na Península Ibérica: Períodos medieval e moderno*, Lisbon, Colibri, Cidehus, Universidad de Alicante, 2008, pp. 259–77.

13. Benjamin Braude, "Cham et Noé: Race, esclavage et exégèse entre islam, judaïsme et christianisme," *Annales: Histoire, sciences sociales*, 2002 (1), pp. 93–125.

14. Karen Ordahl Kupperman, "Presentment of Civility: English Reading of American Self-Presentation in the Early Years of Colonization," *William and Mary Quarterly*, ser. 3, 54 (1), 1997, pp. 193–228.

15. María Elena Martínez, *Genealogical Fictions: Limpieza de Sangre, Religion, and Gender in Colonial Mexico*, Stanford, CA, Stanford University Press, 2008.

16. Robert Bartlett, *The Making of Europe: Conquest, Colonization, and Cultural Change, 950–1350*, Princeton, NJ, Princeton University Press, 1993.

17. Michel Pastoureau, *Noir: Histoire d'une couleur*, Paris, Seuil, "Points Histoire," 2011.

18. Ann Laura Stoler, *Race and the Education of Desire: Foucault's "History of Sexuality" and the Colonial Order of Things*, Durham, NC, Duke University Press, 1995, p. 41, n. 62.

19. David Nirenberg, "El concepto de raza en el estudio del antijudaísmo ibérico medieval," *Edad Media*, 2000, pp. 39–60.

20. Peter Trawny, *Heidegger et l'antisémitisme: Sur les "Cahiers noirs*," Paris, Seuil, 2014, pp. 87–101.

21. Maurice Olender, *Razza e destino*, Milan, Bompiani, 2014, p. 24.

22. Staffan Müller-Wille and Hans-Jörg Rheinberger, eds., *Heredity Produced: At the Crossroads of Biology, Politics, and Culture, 1500–1870*, Cambridge, MA, MIT Press, 2007.

23. Sarah Eigen Figal, *Heredity, Race, and the Birth of the Modern*, New York, Routledge, 2008, p. 12.

24. Roberto Bizzocchi, *Genealogie incredibili: Scritti di storia nell'Europa moderna*, Bologna, Il Mulino, "Annali dell'Istituto storico italo-germanico," 22, 1995; Christiane Klapisch-Zuber, *L'Ombre des ancêtres: Essai sur l'imaginaire médiéval de la parenté*, Paris, Fayard, 2000.

25. Ariela Gross, *What Blood Won't Tell: History of Race on Trial in America*, Cambridge, MA, Harvard University Press, 2008.

26. Naomi Zack, *Race and Mixed Race*, Philadelphia, Temple University Press, 1993, pp. 9–16.

27. Pierre Savy, "Transmission, identité, corruption: Réflexions sur trois cas d'hypodescendance," *L'Homme*, 2007, pp. 53–80.

28. Bruce Baum, *The Rise and Fall of the Caucasian Race: A Political History of Racial Identity*, New York, New York University Press, 2006, p. 22.

29. Ibid., pp. 9–10.

30. Ibid., p. 45ff.

31. Tzvetan Todorov, *On Human Diversity: Nationalism, Racism, and Exoticism in French Thought*, Cambridge, MA, Harvard University Press, "Convergences: Inventories of the Present," 1993, p. 96.

32. Les Back and John Solomos, eds., *Theories of Race and Racism: A Reader*, New York, Routledge, 2001, p. 191.

33. Nicole Lapierre, *Causes communes: Des Juifs et des Noirs*, Paris, Stock, 2011.

34. Enrique Martínez López, *Tablero de ajedrez: Imágenes del negro heroico en la comedia española y en la literatura e iconografía sacra del Brasil esclavista*, Paris, Fondation Calouste Gulbenkian, 1998; David Bindman and Henry Louis Gates Jr., eds., *The Image of the Black in Western Art*, vol. 3, *From the "Age of Discovery" to the Age of Abolition*, Cambridge, MA, Harvard University Press, 2010; Anne Lafont, "La représentation des Noirs: Quel chantier pour l'histoire de l'art?," *Perspective*, 1, 2013, pp. 67–73.

35. Olender, *Race and Erudition*, Cambridge, MA, Harvard University Press, 2009, p. 4; Sander Gilman, "The Jew's Body: Thoughts on Jewish Physical Difference," in Norman L. Kleeblatt, ed., *Too Jewish? Challenging Traditional Identities*, New York, Jewish Museum of New York and Rutgers University Press, 1996, pp. 60–73.

36. Norman Roth, *Conversos, Inquisition, and the Expulsion of the Jews from Spain* (1995), Madison, University of Wisconsin Press, 2002, pp. 230–31.

37. Juan Aranzadi, "Racismo y piedad," in Juan Aranzadi, Jon Juaristi, and Patxo Unzueta, *Auto de terminación (Raza, nación y violencia en el País Vasco)*, Madrid, El País–Aguilar, 1994, p. 36.

38. Danièle Lochak, "La doctrine sous Vichy ou les mésaventures du positivisme," in *Les Usages sociaux du droit*, Paris, Presses universitaires de France, 1989, pp. 250–85; Isabelle Lecoq-Caron, "La preuve de la qualité de juif," *Le Genre humain*, 28, *Juger sous Vichy*, 1994, pp. 41–52.

39. Maurice Duverger, "La situation des fonctionnaires depuis la Révolution de 1940," *Revue du droit public et de la science politique en France et à l'étranger*, 1942, p. 307.

40. Ibid., p. 309.

41. Ibid., p. 307.

42. George Montandon, *Comment reconnaître et expliquer le Juif? Avec dix clichés hors texte suivi d'un portrait moral du Juif*, Paris, Nouvelles Éditions françaises, 1940.

43. Ibid., p. 14.

44. Buffon, *Œuvres*, Paris, Gallimard, "Bibliothèque de la Pléiade," 2007, p. 1024.

45. Jean Marquès-Rivière, *Exposition Le "Juif" et la France au palais Berlitz*, Paris, Institut d'étude des questions juives, 1941. A newsreel filmed on September 12, 1941, http://www.ina.fr/video/AFE86001433/inauguration-de-l-exposition-le-juif-et-la-france-au-palais-berlitz-video.html.

46. Joseph Billig, *L'Institut d'étude des questions juives, officine française des autorités nazies en France: Inventaire commenté de la collection de documents provenant des archives de l'Institut conservés au CDJC*, Paris, CDJC, 1974; Raymond Bach, "Identifying Jews: The Legacy of the 1941 Exhibition, 'Le Juif et la France,'" *Studies in 20th Century Literature*, 23, 1999, pp. 65–92.

47. Doron, *L'homme altéré*, pp. 13–29.

48. Luc Faucher and Édouard Machery, "Construction sociale, biologie et évolution culturelle: Un modèle intégratif de la pensée raciale," in Michel de Fornel and Cyril Lemieux, eds., *Naturalisme versus constructivisme*, Paris, Éditions de l'EHESS, 2008, pp. 213–40; Luc Faucher, *Que sont les races? Essai de métaphysique appliquée*, université du Québec à Montréal, "Les cahiers du LANCI," 2005, p. 4.

49. Hacking, "Why Race," p. 112.

50. W.E.B. Du Bois, *The Souls of Black Folk*, Chicago, A. C. McClurg, 1903, pp. 10–11.

51. Magali Bessone, "W.E.B. Du Bois et la construction des catégories raciales et coloristes dans l'Amérique ségrégationniste," *Nuevos Mundos Mundos Nuevos, Débats*, http://nuevomundo.revues.org/65271.

52. Stephen Cornell and Douglas Hartmann, *Ethnicity and Race: Making Identities in a Changing World*, Thousand Oaks, CA, Pine Forge, 1998, pp. 24–29; Pap N'Diaye, *La Condition noire: Essai sur une minorité française*, Paris, Calmann-Lévy, 2008.

53. Balibar, "Y a-t-il un néo-racisme?"

54. Hebe Maria Mattos, "A escravidão moderna nos quadros do Império português: O Antigo Regime em perspectiva atlântica," in João Fragoso, Maria Fernanda Bicalho, and Maria de Fátima Gouvêa, eds., *O Antigo Regime nos trópicos*, Rio de Janeiro, Civilização Brasileira, 2001, pp. 141–62.

55. Benjamin Braude, "The Sons of Noah and the Construction of Ethnic and Geographical Identities in the Medieval and Early Modern Periods," *William and Mary Quarterly*, ser. 3, 54 (1), 1997, pp. 103–42; Sweet, "Iberian Roots of American Racist Thought."

56. Renato G. Mazzolini, "Il colore della pelle e l'origine dell'antropologia fisica," in Renzo Zorzi, ed., *L'Epopea delle scoperte*, Venise, Olschki, 1994, pp. 229–37; Paola Martínez Pestana, "'Des hommes noirs et non pas des nègres': Piel y raza en el siglo XVIII," *Asclepio*, 63 (1), 2011, pp. 39–64.

57. Lucien Febvre and François Crouzet, *Nous sommes des sang-mêlés: Manuel d'histoire de la civilisation française*, Paris, Albin Michel, 2012.

58. Lucien Febvre, "La voix du sang: Fin d'une mystique?," *Annales: Économies, sociétés, civilisations*, 1949, pp. 149–51.

59. Ashley Montagu, *Man's Most Dangerous Myth: The Fallacy of Race*, New York, Columbia University Press, 1942, p. 42.

60. Madison Grant, *The Passing of the Great Race; or, The Racial Basis of European History*, New York, Charles Scribner's Sons, 1916.

61. Jonathan Peter Spiro, *Defending the Master Race: Conservation, Eugenics, and the Legacy of Madison Grant*, Lebanon, University of Vermont Press, 2009, p. 362; Jean-Louis Vuillierme, *Miroir de l'Occident, le nazisme et la civilisation occidentale*, Paris, Les Éditions du Toucan, 2014, pp. 70–88.

62. Stefan Kühl, *The Nazi Connection: Eugenics, American Racism and German National Socialism*, New York, Oxford University Press, 1994, p. 85.

63. Hans Staden, *Hans Staden's True History: An Account of Cannibal Captivity in Brazil*, Durham, NC, Duke University Press, 2008; Gary L. Ebersole, *Captured by Texts: Puritan to Post-modern Images of Indian Captivity*, Charlottesville, University Press of Virginia, 1995, pp. 15–60; Teresa A. Toulouse, *The Captive's Position: Female Narrative, Male Identity, and Royal Authority in Colonial New England*, Philadelphia, University of Pennsylvania Press, 2006.

64. Ronaldo Vainfas, "Colonização, miscigenação e questão racial: Notas sobre equívocos e tabus da historiografia brasileira," *Tempo*, 8, 1999, pp. 1–12.

65. Charles R. Boxer, *Race Relations in the Portuguese Colonial Empire (1415–1825)*, Oxford, Clarendon, 1963.

66. Alden T. Vaughan, *Roots of American Racism: Essays on the Colonial Experience*, Oxford, Oxford University Press, 1995.

67. Karol Wojtyła, "Address of John Paul II to the International Court of Justice during the Meeting at the Peace Palace," *Insegnamenti di Giovanni Paolo II*, 8 (1), Libreria Editrice Vaticana, 1985, pp. 1313–21.

68. John Connelly, *From Enemy to Brother: The Revolution in Catholic Teaching on the Jews, 1933–1965*, Cambridge, MA, Harvard University Press, 2012, p. 17.

69. Paul Weindling, "Weimar Eugenics: The Kaiser Wilhelm Institute for Anthropology, Human Heredity, and Eugenics in Social Context," *Annals of Science*, 42, 1985, pp. 303–18.

70. John Connelly, "Catholic Racism and Its Opponents," *Journal of Modern History*, 79 (4), 2007, pp. 813–47.

71. Jeffrey M. Shumway, "'The Purity of My Blood Cannot Put Food on My Table': Changing Attitudes towards Interracial Marriage in Nineteenth-Century Buenos Aires," *Americas*, 58 (2), 2001, pp. 201–20.

72. Carolina González Undurraga, "De la casta a la raza: El concepto de raza; Un singular colectivo de la modernidad; México, 1750–1850," *Historia Mexicana*, 60 (3), 2011, pp. 1491–525.

73. Lilia Moritz Schwarcz, *Nem preto nem branco, muito pelo contrário: Cor e raça na sociabilidade brasileira*, São Paulo, Claro Enigma, 2012; Peter Wade, "Racism in Latin America," in Deborah Poole, ed., *A Companion to Latin American Anthropology*, London, Blackwell, 2008, pp. 177–92.

74. Melissa Nobles, "The Myth of Latin American Multiracialism," "On Race," *Daedalus*, 134 (1), 2005, pp. 82–87.

75. Berta Ares Quejía, "Mestizos, mulatos y zambaigos (Virreinato del Perú, siglo XVI)," in Berta Ares Quejía and Alessandro Stella, eds., *Negros, Mulatos, Zam-baigos: Derroteros africanos en los mundos ibéricos*, Seville, Consejo Superior de Investigaciones Científicas, 2000, pp. 76–88; Ana María Presta, "Portraits of Four Elite Women: Traditional Female Roles and Transgressions in Colonial Elite Families in Charcas, 1550–1600," *Colonial Latin American Review*, 9 (2), 2000, pp. 237–62; Jean-Paul Zuniga, "La voix du sang: Du métis à l'idée de métissage en Amérique espagnole," *Annales: Histoire, sciences sociales*, 1999, pp. 425–52.

76. Stolcke, "Los mestizos," pp. 23–25.

77. Fredrickson, *Racism*, p. 21.

78. Stuart B. Schwartz, "La nobleza del mundo nuevo: Movilidad y aspiraciones sociales en la conquista y colonización de la América Española," *Revista de historia*, 8, 1979, http://www.revistas.una.ac.cr/index.php/historia/article/view/2237.

79. Olender, *Race and Erudition*, p. xx; Jonathan Elukin, "From Jew to Christian? Conversion and Immutability in Medieval Europe," in James Muldoon, ed., *Varieties of Religious Conversion in the Middle Ages*, Gainesville, University Press of Florida, 1997, pp. 171–89.

80. Maurice Olender, *Les Langues du paradis: Aryens et Sémites; Un couple providentiel*, Paris, Seuil, "Points Essais," 1989, p. 248.

81. Alexis de Tocqueville, *Democracy in America*, vol. 1, part 2, trans. Gerald Bevan, London, Penguin Classics, 2003, p. 402.

82. Frederick Cooper, Thomas C. Holt, and Rebecca Scott, *Beyond Slavery: Explorations of Race, Labor, and Citizenship in Postemancipation Societies*, Chapel Hill, University of North Carolina Press, 2000.

83. Jean Hébrard and Rebecca Scott, *Freedom Papers: An Atlantic Odyssey in the Age of Emancipation*, Cambridge, MA, Harvard University Press, 2012.

84. Peggy Pascoe, "Miscegenation Law, Court Cases, and Ideologies of 'Race' in Twentieth-Century America," *Journal of American History*, 83 (1), 1996, pp. 44–69, pp. 48–49 cited here; George Fredrickson, *White Supremacy: A Comparative Study in American and South African History*, New York, Oxford University Press, 1981, pp. 99–108.

85. Léon Poliakov, *The History of Anti-Semitism*, vol. 3, *From Voltaire to Wagner*, trans. Miriam Kochan, Philadelphia, University of Pennsylvania Press, 2003, p. 309.

86. Michel Leiris, *Race and Culture*, Paris, Unesco, 1951, pp. 6–7. For an analysis of the period of 1945–52 and its middle-term repercussions, in regards to Claude Lévi-Strauss, see Wiktor Stoczkowski, "Racisme, antiracisme et cosmologie lévi-straussienne: Un essai d'anthropologie réflexive," *L'Homme*, 182, 2007, pp. 7–51.

Conclusion. Race and Sameness

1. Vincent Descombes, *Les Embarras de l'identité*, Paris, Gallimard, 2013, pp. 186–96.

2. Boas, *Race*, p. 11.

3. Anténor Firmin, *The Equality of the Human Races: Positivist Anthropology*, trans. Asselin Charles, Champaign, University of Illinois Press, 2002, p. 152.

4. Boas, *Race*, pp. 8–9.

5. Ibid., p. 10.

6. Ibid., p. 192.

7. Ibid., p. 171.

INDEX

[200] INDEX

Doron, Claude-Olivier, 41, 74–75,
154
Du Bois, W.E.B., 155–56
Duverger, Maurice, 148–49

Efron, Noah, 55–56
Elias, Norbert, 130
ensavagement, 160
Entine, Jon, 49
Erasmus, Desiderius, 62
essentialism, 49, 56, 65
Essner, Cornelia, 120
ethnic cleansing. See genocide
ethnocentrism, 108, 143, 148
eugenics, 28, 45, 102, 115, 159
Eurocentrism, 142
evolution, 37, 45, 50, 99, 108, 128,
133–34

Fanon, Frantz, 5, 36, 61–62
Farris, Nancy, 27
Fassin, Didier, 32
Febvre, Lucien, 159
femininity stigma, 96, 99–100
Ferguson, Adam, 80
Ferguson, R. Brian, 52–55
Fields, Barbara Jeanne, 97
Figal, Sarah Eigen, 138–39
Firmin, Anténor, 175
Flem, Lydia, 65
Forza Nuova, 60
Foucault, Michel, 122, 131, 135
France: racism in, 4–5, 14–15, 29–
33, 47, 59. See also "race" term
avoidance
Frankel, Charles, 46
Frederickson, George M., 82, 142–43,
167–68
Freud, Sigmund, 65
Freyre, Gilberto, 164

Galen, 20, 111
genetics, 2–3, 12–13, 21, 31, 43–49,
54, 58, 67, 74–75, 112, 115, 120,
138, 173; Nazi rejection of, 26–27,
172. See also heredity and lineage
genocide, 4, 13, 45, 88, 115–17, 120
Genre humain, Le, 46
Gide, André, 4
Gliozzi, Giuliano, 35, 96
Gobineau, Arthur de, 28, 103
Godwin's law, 25
Goffman, Erving, 92
Göring, Hermann, 172
Gorky, Maxim, 116
Grant, Madison, 159–60
GRECE (Research and Study Group
for European Civilization), 46
Gross, Ariela, 139
Grossman, Vasily, 116–17
Guamán Poma de Ayala, Felipe, 36

Hacking, Ian, 113, 154–55
Haitian Revolution, 146
Hartmann, Douglas, 156
Hébrard, Jean, 170
Hegel, Georg Wilhelm Friedrich, 168
Heidegger, Martin, 136, 137
heredity and lineage, 9, 12–13, 17,
21, 26–27, 29, 38–39, 58, 66, 77,
78, 83–84, 101, 111, 125, 132–33,
134, 137–40, 148, 153; aristocracy
and, 39, 128–29; Grossman on,
117
Hering Torres, Max, 99, 126
Herodotus, 20, 124
Hespanha, António Manuel, 95–96
Hippocrates, 20, 111
Hitler, Adolf, 117, 160
Hollande, François, 29
Holocaust, 3–4, 88, 172
homophobia, 9, 11, 92
human genome mapping, 27, 44

Ibrahim, Awad, 62
Identitaires, 6
identity, 9, 16, 22, 65, 107–8. See also
self-identification

A NOTE ON THE TYPE

{⚊⚊⚊⚊⚊}

THIS BOOK has been composed in Miller, a Scotch Roman typeface designed by Matthew Carter and first released by Font Bureau in 1997. It resembles Monticello, the typeface developed for The Papers of Thomas Jefferson in the 1940s by C. H. Griffith and P. J. Conkwright and reinterpreted in digital form by Carter in 2003.

Pleasant Jefferson ("P. J.") Conkwright (1905–1986) was Typographer at Princeton University Press from 1939 to 1970. He was an acclaimed book designer and AIGA Medalist.

The ornament used throughout this book was designed by Pierre Simon Fournier (1712–1768) and was a favorite of Conkwright's, used in his design of the *Princeton University Library Chronicle*.